AT THE CROSS

POEMS BY

SETH IRVING

authorHOUSE®

AuthorHouse™
1663 Liberty Drive
Bloomington, IN 47403
www.authorhouse.com
Phone: 833-262-8899

Published by AuthorHouse 08/26/2021

ISBN: 978-1-6655-3636-3 (sc)
ISBN: 978-1-6655-3635-6 (e)

Library of Congress Control Number: 2021917582

Print information available on the last page.

Contents

Dedication xiii

CHAPTER 1
At the Cross

A Heart for God's Correction.. 1
What Price Did He Pay? 2
Why Would He Do it?... 3
The Meekest of Men 4
We Need Only One 5
Trails of Fire... 6
I Have a Dream... 7
Falling for The Hype 9
Yes! I Am a Christian… 10
Dying In This World, Living on This Planet 11
No Good Thing... 12
Hero.. 13
Fallen Giant 14
The Word Is a Two-Edged Sword.. 15

CHAPTER 2
The Love of a Father

All I Ever Knew 19
My Boy.. 21
All It Takes 22
The Way of a Father.. 24
A Voice from The Deep 25

God's Voice Echoes the Generations 26

When God Revealed to Us His Son 27

Thank You for Being Persistent 28

Memory Lane... 29

The Iron Gate 30

The Working Man's Wisdom 31

Father of Greatness.. 32

Perfection's in My Way... 33

CHAPTER 3

Inspirations and Motivations

To Hell with Good Intensions.. 37

The Slow Death of Trying... 38

You're Becoming Michal Jordan Through that Pen 40

Let the Wind Carry Your Hope 42

In the Morning 43

I Smell Smoke 44

Love Makes Us Courageous 45

Seeing The Invisible 46

I Know Everything, and That's Why I'm Still Learning..................... 48

You Are the Exception... 49

By Means Of Many Wonders 51

Our Future Forever 52

I Have an idea 53

I Write Poetry That Makes Me Afraid to Write more........................ 54

Pleasure Beyond Comprehension 55

My World 56

The Strength of The Truth Is the Arm of The Lord............................ 58

The Great Part About the Gospel.. 59

Let Things Go as They Should 61

Curse Breaker.. 62

A Dead-Letter 63

Jealousy Is a Powerful Motivator 64

There Is Power in The Truth... 66

God Will Make a Way 68

But first, You Must Believe.. 69

Just By Faith 70

For Every Circle, There's A Square 72

Shining in the dark 74

Get knocked Down: Stand Back Up! 75

My Story the Talk of The Town 76

Born from Necessity.. 77

The Darkest Paths Are Preserved for The Brightest Lights 78

The Strength I Need from Day to Day.. 80

Comfort Ye 81

It's Empowering to Empower You 82

I Gotta Keep Writing.. 84

Where The Finest Are Made 85

Till the Ground.. 86

We Can Save The World.. 87

A Powerful People 90

Go with Them 91

Write Away the Pain.. 93

The Freedom of The Fall 95

The Things we Walk Through Yet Don't Know the Answer To.......... 96

Life 98

Dream On Dreamer.. 100

CHAPTER 4

Black Man

The First Born of The World 103

How Did You Get Here? 104

The Glory of His People... 107

Just Check Your History 108

Soldiers On a Different Battlefield 109

Jordans In Jail 111

Time is money, bruh! You ain't heard?..112

Always Be Brothers 113

Let Me Through 114

You're Gonna Prove Em' All Wrong 117

Jesus Lifted the Ghetto with All the Strength of His Soul................. 119
Hard Work Builds Character 120
The Gangster in Him Had To, The Saint in Him Was Sad To 122
Lock Away Another Brilliant Mind.. 124
For Reasons, We Hope to See... 127
The Wicked Will Vanish.. 128
In A World Gone Mad Wanders a Madman Lost............................ 129
I Just Bumped My Head on The Ceiling, and It Hurts! 131
It's Hard to Be Humble and Cocky at The Same Time 133
In Time, All Things Will Be Perfected Because Your Timing is
Perfect 134
Unto The Promise... 136

CHAPTER 5
The Living Word

He Guards His Word with His Life 139
The Promise is Real 140
When the Truth Comes Along... 142
Jesus Felt Alone 144
He Made It Understandable 145

CHAPTER 6
Living in Sin

Faint Hearts Cry...149
Ties..150
Happy 151
The Silent Suffer 152
A Fools Promise 153
Transgression 154
Only God Can Judge Me...155
Why Do I doubt 156
It Feels Good to Cry 157
Angry Fool..159
Payback.. 160

Submission...161
Satan Disguised as God...162
The True Exploiters of Grace 163
Docile Brows...164
Playing With Fire...165
Behold, The Shattered Remains of a Broken Man...........................166
Lord, Make Me A Better Man...167
False Believe...168
Inside I'm Crying...170
Oh, Wretched Man..171
Stumbling Block 173
If You're Not Being Tested 174
Prisoner of The Mind..175
The Test of a Man 177
Talking Up a Storm 178

CHAPTER 7

Testify

Suicide Prevention..181
You Can Take My Life, but You Can't Take My Purpose. 182
You Made Me Live 183
Temptation...185
Tears Of Joy 186
You Are with Me..188
God Is Always with Me...190
God, You're My Only Friend...191
I Got Here by His Grace...192

CHAPTER 8

Church Hurt

Church Hurt...197
Oh, Thirsty Soul..198
Friends Fade Away 199
Where The Road Ends..200

Some People, You Don't Want in Your Life 201
It's A Full-Time Job Keeping Hate Out of Your Heart...................... 202
The Truth Will Set You Free... 204
Mercy Is a Choice 205
Misleading Light.. 207
Let Us Break Bread Together on Our Knees 209
Throwing Stones...210
Forgive Them..212
Level The Playing Field..213
Get On My Level..215

CHAPTER 9

Closer than a Brother

The Fairest Thing to Do is to Be Unfair 219
The Greatest Power Is Love... 221
The People You Love... 222

CHAPTER 10

Recollection of Revelation

What Is Hidden in The Light of God?... 225
Our Spirit is Covered in Dirt 226
As We Get Older, We Make Mistakes.. 227
Stars 229
You Are One of The Stars 230
Never Thought of It That Way 231
My Mind is Changing the World, but This World is Not
Changing My Mind.. 232
My God is Indestructible 233
Take the Top Off Your Faith.. 234
The Love That Comes from God.. 236
Lost Soul.. 237
Time 238
The Audacity to Ask, The Audacity to Expect 239
Role Play.. 240

Where the Universe Ends, Our Being Begins.................................... 241
When The Creator Calls.. 242
Everything Hangs by A Hair of Faith 243
There's Always Space for More Ideas.. 244
Those Fearful Moments Can Be Humbling, and Those
Humbling Moments Can Be Fearful.. 245

CHAPTER 11

The End

The Last but Not the Least, The Least but Not the Last.................. 249
Make Ready a Path for Our God 251
He Is a Holy God..252
We Did Not Come from Animals.. 254
There is Hope for The World.. 256
The World Needs Love 257
Bullies eventually Get Bullied 258
Passion 259
World War 260
Sins Blind a Man.. 261
It's Just a Matter of Time... 263
Does The Sun Hurt Your Eyes?...264
America is Standing on a Giant Trap 265
When the mountains Fall.. 267
The World's Last Judge 269
The Wise will be Waiting... 271
The Day the World Hates Love... 272
Is it Written? 274

CHAPTER 12

The World Upside Down

The Peculiar People... 279
That Is the Hope We Share.. 280
Estranged of Men.. 282
Poor Blind Sheep.. 283

Everything Is Nothing to Me 284

Everything Is Fading at The Crust 285

The American Dream Must Die 286

Honor The Fallen Heroes... 288

The Shame of the Nation 290

Trouble..291

CHAPTER 13

Perfect Love

Paradox 295

The Perfect Mirror 296

I Plead the Blood... 297

Love Without Conditions.. 298

Levels Of Compassion and Depths to Mercy 300

Know Your Worth.. 301

Dedication

I dedicate this book to a man who I've watched carry 'his cross' every day of my life. I could not be half the man I am today if it were not for this one man's shining example of what it means to be a father. I never saw him do anything that he didn't want 'us', his children, doing my entire life.

Growing up my father was a remarkable example of what it means to be a great father. He set and upheld a standard for loving and honoring God as long as I can remember. He taught me my appreciation for the 'Word of God'. As a kid I'd stumble in on him all the time alone in his room reading his 'word' and the only time we missed church was when we were having it right at home lol. He was never too proud to say 'I'm sorry' or admit when he had made a mistake. He was a father who believed in forgiveness. He not only told us that the word "can't" should never be in a man's vocabulary, but he showed us as well. He did what seemed impossible as if it were nothing, and to me and my brothers and sisters, he was the REAL-LIFE SUPER MAN lol... He wore so many different hats growing up (business owner, deacon in the church, die hard roller skater etc..) but he incorporated his family in everything he ever did and we came second to nothing, but God himself... If that wasn't enough, he wasn't just a father to me and my siblings, but he fathered every lost child he came into contact with. He taught so many of us 'the game' in my neighborhood and community, not with words alone, but by ACTIONS. He took so many under his wing while still taking care of his own responsibilities. Truly the older I get the smarter he looks in my eyes. Everything I am I owe to this man, and words cannot express how humbled I am to call him my father...

CHAPTER 1

At the Cross

A Heart for God's Correction

Vain repetitious beating,
vicious, malicious swinging,
skin hanging, strength failing;
precious life depleting…
All this for a sin that had yet to be committed,
all this for a sin that had yet to be remitted.
A lowly proof, a higher lesson,
a humble heart for God's correction…
Precious love,
precious loss,
precious blood,
rugged cross…

What Price Did He Pay?

He paid the price for eternal life: well, what price did he pay;
what were the chances that he took in showing us the way?
The burden of eternal life, how much does it weigh?
He paid the price for eternal life but, what price did he pay?
We all know the answer is blood, sweat, and tears;
we all *know* but will not *show* the sum of all of our fears...
But this one man faced his demons squared-up, ready to fight!
Now, tell me, what type of push does it take to make the **truth** come to light?
Tell me, what could motivate one to purchase eternal life,
lay it all on the line and pay the ultimate price?
You could say that the ultimate price is the price for eternal life
because, ultimately, *life* is eternally priced...

To give sight to sore eyes, he was a sore eye's sight,
and one must die the ultimate death to live the *eternal life*.
Amazingly, though, he died as a show;
demonstrating *the way* as the light of the globe;
showing off his crown, revealing a heart of gold;
now the price for eternal life is as a love story told...

Why Would He Do it?

Why would he do it?
Why would he go through it?
How much is a nail in your hand worth?
How much for two?
How much to nail his feet through?
On the cross, he bargained for the church;
he paid the price for us to know our worth!
When you look down on yourself,
do you know how that hurts?

Look in the mirror and love your reflection;
see the beauty of who you are: no more regretting!
Turn the page, and start a new day in full view of his love for you;
look at the price that he paid...

The Meekest of Men

God fashioned him in a way that would never offend,
but his rise to power would be gracious, as the meekest of men.

One who holds a position, not of his own will
but, in the knowledge of a divine purpose, he serves with such zeal!

His words were weighty because his truth was real;
a man of influence and power moved deeply to feel
the iniquities of his subjects to level the field,
as the meekest of men, upon eternity, build!

Rarely do we regard men of lowly-estate;
we figure anyone with power would surely be great
but, behold, this man lives solely to serve;
his rise to greatness and power ascribe to his word!
As his honor, he lays down, and his glory he gives to others
he vindicates equality and deems us all brothers…

Though some would seek out their own attention and importance
among men
God fashioned him in a way that would never offend,
but his rise to power would be gracious, as the meekest of men.

We Need Only One

We need only one man of nine billion and ten
to stand up against the world,
to change the world within...

We need only one man
unafraid to truly, TRULY, go against the grain;
though he is trampled by an angry mob
the world will never be the same!

Yes, the whole world can be against him;
his hope will shine forth as the sun,
lighting upon the planet:
of all men, we need only one...
to alter the past from the day in which man began;
only one man...
to change the future and the way that it all should end.

They say it's hard making a difference,
but, oh, how the difference is 'hardly done';
outnumbered by the world,
now the 'world' have we become...

Is there any brave man, any courageous or daring son
willing to stand up to the world?
we need only one...

Trails of Fire

I walk with footsteps as trails of fire;
burning within my heart is the Lord's desire!
Oblivious to my fate consumed by his will,
I shall fear no evil but have nerves of steel!

I Have a Dream

"I have a dream!"
said the king as he spoke through a human being,
"That one day chains would shatter, and freedom would ring!"

In honor of this man and the message that he sent,
should we all fall to our knees and sincerely repent!
We must redirect our views to an alignment of clues
that may inspire revelation to the coming good news!
Shall we boycott and protest to an 'unchanging hand'
or submit to the divine nature of a glorious plan.
Surely, we shall all be hated for his name,
but shall we give our lives to hatred and bring his name Shame?
Forgiveness is the only way; in the way of wisdom is peace:
to accept the unacceptable and trust that change will not cease!
It's been a long time coming, but I know that 'a change gon come.'
He will give sight to the blind; he will give sense to the dumb!
There has never been a minute when his love was *not* in control,
but in his suffering and patience, he does what's best for the whole.
Therefore, put down your strife's and let go of contention;
all shall be well once this dream has been finished!
Give in to those who hate you, let them know that you care,
suffer them to take your loved ones as you have plenty to spare!
Weeping may endure for a night, but joy comes in the morning;
lay your burdens at the sun and give way to his coming.
Although he seems so far away, all is drawing near to him:
to his love, to his patients, to his completion of the end.
Behold, in this dream, he makes all things new!
Please don't be stubborn to change but let *him* change *you*...

Love those that hate you, pray for them that misuse you;
endure shame for his honor, uphold those that accuse you!
Soon we will say to death, "where is your sting,"
and to the grave, we shall say, "there is no more to bring."
Then the king shall finally rest once he has finished his dream,
and his word shall be rest for all human beings.
When, finally, the chains are broken, on that day we shall sing,
and in the holiness of his presence,
freedom shall ring!

Falling for The Hype

If you're feeling quite offended, rather black or white,
if you feel the need to do something, rather wrong or right,
there may be a slight chance that they've tricked your sight
by instigating to the point that you fell for the hype!
Is it just me, or weren't we friends just three years ago?
Why, in one year, did all the differences show?
Just so happens, our conflict came when we were nearing the end;
it seems they'd rather we die enemies before we die friends.
Michael said it doesn't matter if you're black or white;
now Michaels dead, but the truth is still giving him life...
I know they hurt you badly, but please don't fight,
I know they did you wrong, but please don't strike.
Forgive and forget, and move on with life;
count not any sin for Jesus paid the price.
Just forgive and forget and move on with life;
stay grounded in the truth, do not excite.
We are all God's children, and it starts with Christ,
so remember who you are before you fall for the hype...

Yes! I Am a Christian...

To say that I am a Christian is to say that I believe in Christ;
that there is a risen savior given the keys to death and life.
So, should the question present itself,
by any means, I will not fail to mention
that I believe in God's salvation:
so yes, I am a Christian!

In a room full of people doomed to be slaughtered,
please, do kill me first; by death, I won't be bothered.
If 'you taking my life' helps you make your decision,
rather or not, to believe in Christ: then yes, I am a Christian!

Because many seek after Christ while it is Christ they reject,
to prove his love for you, I will give my last breath...
Are you curious to know my faith? Do you wonder its depths?
If you're asking if I'm a Christian, well, the answer is yes.

In a world where everyone seeks to save their own life,
in a world where death is real, but few can see Christ,
I must hold true to my confession that a savior makes me right,
even in my death, I must bring this to light...

So, should the question present itself,
by any means, I will not fail to mention
that I believe in God's salvation:
so yes, I am a Christian!

Dying In This World, Living on This Planet

What God has made for good man has used for bad,
so while I'm happy I was created, my existence here is sad.
Finding the purpose for my life is the conflict that I have,
for should I do what's right I'll have reason to be glad,
but should I do what's wrong, I'll have reason to be mad.

God encourages me, saying,
"Do not give up on yourself,
you're not in this world alone,
you will always have my help."

The devil discourages me, saying,
"You were meant for evil!
There's no hope for this planet
for I control the people!"

A choice is what I have; a decision is what he gave
to create the finished product and to define the thing he's made.
Should I trust in this world and give it my very soul,
it will consume me in its passions and swallow us as a whole,
but if I put my trust in God and the gift that he gave,
I'll bring healing to this planet and prove the power to save!
The creating is left to me now; the creation, have I been handed;
I'm fighting for my life now, with every seed that God has planted.
At times, life is a struggle; at times, my soul seems stranded
dying in this world, living on this planet.

No Good Thing

Of a truth, there is no good thing;
name one solid rock of which my soul should cling!
Everything that matters doesn't matter, and every mountain is dust;
oh, what vanity awaits those who walk the earth's crust!
Indeed, these words are heavier than the matters that be;
as the earth is to water, they are as deep as the sea.
So also, is 'my reason' to this 'corruptible green.'
Tell me, what then is secure when there is no good thing?
This world is no more real than the most vivid dream.
Only a fool would love this life with contentment and glee
expecting, not destruction, but fulfillment in things.
I should live this life in fear, for in what shall I hope?
Should I live in expectation, I shall live in reproach.
Every day is dark and distorted with doubt.
My only hope in this life is that one day I make it out!
Of a truth, all is false, and this truth I revere,
that in light of all I see no good thing is here…
All that awaits me is traps; all that elates me is snares
to carry me far, far away with this world and its cares.
Should one delight himself in idols
should one make covenants with death;
so also, are the dealings of this world made to our last breath!
Oh, the day that all is gone, on this day I shall sing,
when all traps have been trapped with no false thing to cling.
Then and only then we'll see…
Of a truth, there is no good thing!

Hero

Inside of everyone lives a hero; the spirit is there!
It calls out to many, but few truly care:
the desire to save greater than the desire to consume;
the heart of a man to stand faced with certain doom.
There is no greater motivation than the one from above;
when one digs deep within to find the power of love.
In the gut of his stomach lives the greatness of glory,
inside the very heart of a man, a victorious story.
With great care for his cause and compassion-unknown,
he does the impossible to write what is wrong.
Though many stand against him, none are as sure
as the one who stands alone with a heart that is pure.
He will not look left or right, but his eyes are affixed;
knowing what lies in the balance, his soul is convinced.
All factors and variables add up to zero.
He is at peace with himself,
inside him is a hero!

Fallen Giant

What remains of the fallen giant?
Massive muscles now lay silent;
what once was boisterous: a mighty roar,
is now, for birds, meat galore!
Its strength scatters across the fields
till big dry bones lie stiff and still.
What once trampled mere men as bugs
now the insects share as grubs.
As its corps decay upon the ground,
there, flowers spring where it fell down.
Yes, jubilant praise from shades of violet
arise amidst the fallen giant…

The Word Is a Two-Edged Sword

I shall go to war with this to edge sword;
may the righteous be healed, may the wicked be destroyed!
Wounded and defeated is the army I raise.
We cling to the truth to the end of our days!
Yielding the word of God, at the end of our blade
is the piercing of the heart, is the power that saves!
Yes, I shall go to war with this two-edged sword!

CHAPTER 2

The Love of a Father

All I Ever Knew

Growing up, you were all I ever knew;
I didn't know good so, for good I followed you.
I walked in your steps, trailed in your paths,
followed your very will and did as you asked.
I picked up from you my walk,
I picked up from you my talk,
I gathered from you my mind,
from you my train of thought.
No, I couldn't tell the difference
and the difference I never knew
between my friends without a father
and me who had you…
Still, you stayed patient in your going
as if one day surely knowing
that everything I'd learn to do
was right there in your showing.
I watched many friends go astray,
not knowing of their way,
some dying before their time
having not the time of day.
While as yet you read your word,
while as yet you kneeled to pray,
while as yet I watched and learned
what to do and what to say.
Today I am a man full and grown
yet, still learning how you did
all of the things that were shown.
Although now we grow apart

as I stand on my own.
Although we take a different path now
into the unknown.
One thing's for sure in all that I do,
the heart of me will not be far
from all that I ever knew.

My Boy

My boy is a delight to me,
the sun each day exciting me.
Since his birth I've been reborn,
his life restores the fight in me!
I feel so whole, I feel complete
when we're together and our eyes meet,
there's nothing better than when we greet!
I fall to my knees; he runs to me.
In my arms, he holds me strong;
within this love, there is no wrong.
His imagination does create me;
captivated his spirit takes me.
This boy of mine is mighty fine,
and life with him elates me!

All It Takes

All it takes is a little fire,
a little faith to inspire.

Now, I may not have it all, but I'll pass down to him what I can;
a mustard seed, so small, will I place in the palm of his hand.
I will give unto him what I've got even though it's not a lot
and I won't worry if he's got a shot
as long as I bring to him what was brought…
Because all it takes is a little fire a little faith to inspire;
because all it takes is a little hope, I'll give to him all that I know.

One man heaps up a wealth of riches to pass down to his son,
another heaps up a wealth of faith to the ends of a story begun.

One man passes down his power in the form of earthly gain,
another man sends down a shower of wisdom from his pain.

Now, who knows what becomes of the two sons;
rather sunshine come or rain…
Rather one be foolish, or one be wise,
only time can make it plain…

No, I may not have it all, but I'll pass down to him what I can.
Yes, a mustard seed, so small, will I place in the palm of his hand.

Just a breath of life and a little dirt take the form of a man.
Yes, an honest heart, a faithful hope, and to his feet he'll stand.

Because all it takes is a little hope, I'll give to him all that I know.

My earnest gift: his **true** desire;
all it takes is a little fire,
a little faith to inspire.

The Way of a Father

He is their protector as their little eyes behold;
the giant towering over them whose way is sure as gold.
They know nothing of the evil forces beyond his reach,
for he is diligent to watch over them, should *his way* they safely keep.
Strong and sturdy, muscles bulging, he stands-guard their life's unfolding.
For the tenderness of their innocence would be as a hopeless dream
should they take on the world around them without the protection of
their king.
He is a boundary for their existence,
the only thing standing between them and certain doom…
He guards their way; a trail he'll blaze, as for them he makes room.
No, they know nothing of the evil forces beyond his reach,
for he is diligent to watch over them, should *his way* they safely keep.
Yes, he is their protector as their little eyes behold;
the giant towering over them whose way is sure as gold!
Such is the way of all life,
from the day in which life 'begun'.
Such is the way of a father
in the way he raise a son.

A Voice from The Deep

A deep voice echoes and resounds throughout eternity:
a voice from the deep has no ends for which it speaks,
its meaning is for the interpretation of eternity;
it means something different to each generation,
giving its meaning an eternal interpretation;
it grows in significance and, with time, demands more appreciation…

Who can understand the true meaning of the words that come from such
a deep voice?
Who can interpret the ends of such a profound word choice?

His voice is as the 'sound of many waters':
whoever could drink every drip of both the ocean and the sea,
wouldn't even come close to understanding a **word** from a voice from the
deep.

At such bass, the earth quakes, and the establishment shakes
so that mere men should tremble as a drum vibrates…

so deep is the tone from the sound of his hum
that the song he is singing over men can rarely be sung…

With much fear and trembling would every tongue, nation, and tribe
kneel at his feet
before man ever begin to understand a **word** from a *voice from the deep…*

God's Voice Echoes the Generations

The same thing God is telling you, guess what: he told your momma too!
His voice echoes the generations; he tells them through and through.
What he says is not only for today but for many years to come;
he even speaks out from the grave for those whose life is done.
Your ancestors before you, beg and plead with God
that the sins of their life be stopped within your time.
We serve a faithful God and so he speaks through and through,
now the same thing he told your father is the same thing he's telling you!

The curse is broken, you are free; obey the voice of God.
No longer be deceived; forsake this life of lies.
As your generation come, so shall your generation go.
You shall soon see the fruits of the life in which you sow...

Listen to God, I pray, for he's speaking day-to-day
that you may change your ways from those who don't obey.
Obedience is the key to ending your soul's frustration.
Even your ancestors would agree; God's voice echoes the generations.

When God Revealed to Us His Son

———— ✦ ————

When God revealed to us his son, he undid the world's very first sin,
he broke the curse from long ago that made us into mere men.
When God revealed to us his son, he drew out of man his purpose,
yes, the power that is deep within a man he brought it right up to the
surface!

See, it takes more than a mere man to break the chains,
so he showed *man* to be *God*, and he showed *God* to *save*...

When God revealed to us his son, *to us*, a son was revealed to God:
one made in his image, of whom it was no surprise
that unto God he would be *like*, that he would be *like* unto God...

As a father cheers his son after hitting his first home run,
"That's my boy!" said God when Jesus said, "It is done..."
and as his body hang **limp**, as his bloody frame **drip**,
God stood there proud with his hand on his hip.

Adam indeed was pure without sin, and he alone was the *first one*...
but even Adam wasn't deemed worthy of being called *God's son*...

See, when God revealed to us his son, he undid the world's very first sin;
he broke the curse from long ago the made us into mere men...

Thank You for Being Persistent

Thank you for being persistent!
My life's existence is because of your decision to be persistent…
For those times when you came to visit,
called my phone, and I must have missed it;
thank you for being persistent!
For those times when I was down, and you still came around
and had the nerve to ask, "What is it?"
Thank you for being persistent!

My life is full of qualities like you…
because you stuck around with me like we were **glued**.

And rather I knew or not to go the distance
you still took the time to be persistent.
Thank you for being persistent…

Memory Lane

I remember days like this back when I was a kid.
I guess not a lot has changed; you've been the same ever since.
Still taking the same routes, still carrying the same loads,
still struggling to get there; the only difference is that now we're old...
I remember back when we had dreams to make it big;
you were in your prime, and I was just a kid.
However, now we seldom speak, now it is what it is;
those dreams still distant cousins from the day-to-day we live.
I've learned over the years, and I hope you have too
what it takes to fail your plans and make a dream come true.
Now I must admit, it's kind of sad what we still do:
same hustle, same struggle, still the same me and you...
I wonder if things will finally be different this go-round.
I'm trying my best to be positive, not to let your hopes down.
All I know, as on we go, is that not a lot has changed;
it just reminds me of the past, to go down memory lane...

The Iron Gate

Every morning that I wake, I dread the iron gate.
It reminds me of my fate, enslaved to a life I hate.
Burdened by its weight and its stubborn rusty make,
I struggle in my push to start another weary day.
Enthusiasm leaves me, and I fail to appreciate
the chance to live out a life burdened in such a state.
Maybe I am ungrateful and foolish in my complaints;
maybe I should be thankful and not wasteful in 'little things.'
Truly, I cannot hide the hatred I feel inside
toward the burden of my beating, knowing the pain will not subside.
Truly, I'd have lied to say I'm happy when I'm not,
that I enjoy the day-to-day struggle nonstop.

The Working Man's Wisdom

Beneath the pride of men is the work of the heart within;
toil and *grind* strive for a sign beneath the surface of skin.
At **heart**, we are all men.
At **heart,** our work must begin.
So in oil and grime, hard work do we find to prove the heart that's within.

The Man stands tall in his tower; *cleanliness,* claim to his power.
He will pick not an ax and lift not a shovel,
his heart lifted high from the trouble of rubble;
but at the sway of his hand, the decree of his pen;
at his command, the work must begin.

Now his mind is at work to be sure,
as he fashions his heart to be pure;
that beneath the surface of skin
is the work of the heart within.

Dare I say it...

but the burden is equally 'bared'
and the work is equally shared
for at **heart** the work must begin
and at **heart**, we are all men...

Father of Greatness

There is no father like the father of greatness;
careful in his love, with perfection he shapes us.
More than an earthly father: from moderation, he breaks us.
He expects so much more as the father of greatness.
He pushes us to our limits purging our very core,
redefining our minds to reach for so much more.
In mediocracy, his heart will never settle;
away from regularity, he pushes us to the pedal.
Though we want to blend in, he won't let us be devils
but insists again and again that all his children are special.
He examines us thoroughly and compares us to him;
because we're made in his image, we can never grow dim.
He inspires us to be 'fires' that blaze through the night.
Overcoming all darkness: the fears and the fright.
He makes us courageous; he turns 'us' to 'him';
he trains us for greatness, to be more than mere men!
Often, we get discouraged in how long it will take us;
often, our strength fails as, often, he breaks us.
But we must be mindful of the father that shapes us,
that he is no normal father, but the father of greatness!

Perfection's in My Way

I'm in the struggle of my life, and it's a battle every day;
I'm in a fight against the odds because perfection's in my way!
I cannot make my way around it; I must face my greatest fears!
I must stand up to 'perfection' and see it for what it is!
So what, if it beats me down! So what, if it breaks me!
I've been waiting **all of my life** to see what it **makes me**!
Though a part of me wants to cry, shrivel up, and die,
the heart of me will not lie; I still believe that I can fly!

Through trials and tribulations, Lord grant me the patience;
as I get weak in the way, help me reach my destination!
They say that *no one's perfect*, but I am *not* just *any-one;*
my relation to perfection is as a father to his *son.*
The struggle is real, what more can I say?
Despite how I feel, I get stronger each day!
There's no comfort where I'm at, but you coerce me to stay
I must try, although to lose is okay...
I'm in the struggle of my life and it's a battle each day.
I'm in a fight against the odds because perfection's in my way!

CHAPTER 3

Inspirations and Motivations

To Hell with Good Intensions

You can't trust the heart,
to hell with good intensions!

Wishful thinking has got me nothing;
my prayers an empty promise.

I've been hoping all for nothing,
but I've done nothing to be honest.
Truth be told, I've been talking and not walking with my vision;
my heart is good, but I can't trust it, so to hell with good intensions!

If the road to hell is paved with these
then the only way that I'll see heaven
is if I put these plans into action
and, towards my goals, get to stepping!
Cause I'm pretty sure God needs a body,
I'll do his will with these hands and feet,
loving not in words alone but also in truth and deed.
Ima line my plans up with his so he can work beside me;
doing what is pleasing in his sight is something pleasing to see.
Finally, it's my decision rather or not I fail the mission;
when I'm sending up these prayers,
if they be more than good intension…

The Slow Death of Trying

I once knew a friend who didn't do it but tried,
he gave what had seemed his best, but before 'doing' he died.
So many dreams he had that never came true
because 'trying' was not enough if never would he do.

See, in his mind, he had made it up;
he was convinced that he would fail.
Now, 'trying' was just a word he used
for things he could not tell…

His death was slow indeed
his life seemed not to last;
he lived in fear of his future
haunted by an angry past…

Although he had many dreams of his future
of which he saw himself flying
his reality was full of bleakness
as the slow death of trying…

You see, 'trying' is a word used by those who refuse to do,
it's like a 'maybe' instead of yes or no, or an 'I guess' with no clue…

Because 'trying' was all he had for hope,
'doing,' he would never say.
Now, under this false sense of security
his hope could not stay…

His passion and zeal, while feeling real,
would someday dwindle away;

his friends would hate to see him fail,
"try harder," they'd say...
but failure was on his lips
in the words he would say...

Truly, nothing is worse than a slow death in dying;
truly, nothing's more cursed than the sad truth of 'trying'...

You're Becoming Michal Jordan Through that Pen

You're becoming Michael Jordan through that pen;
writing to gain the knowledge of the power that's within!
When you step on that ball court, they all know your name:
shaking in their tennis shoes, terrified that you might play your game!
See, for you to express yourself is for them to bear their shame;
unstoppable on the court, they can't help but feel your pain!

Yeah, you're becoming Michael Jordan through that pen;
writing to gain the knowledge of the power that's within!

Ink drops from the ball-point like sweat from the brow;
first one to draw blood, last one to foul...

Passion consumes you in your will to discover yourself,
so you lay it ALL on the floor; you want your soul to be FELT!

You refuse to be unsure of the power that lies within
because nerves of steel never break, and iron-will NEVER bends!

But with a pencil and paper, you put your heart to the test
knowing that if you gave your heart, surely, you gave your best!

The way you handle the rock like Picasso handles a brush;
silence moves over the crowd right before the flush...
Fingers in poised position as the ball enters the net;
you impress upon the world moments they won't forget!

You inspire them to greatness because your game is a work of art;
beautiful in its time, a masterpiece of the heart!

Writing to gain the knowledge of the power that's within;
to lose you cannot fathom, to know yourself is a WIN!

It's no wonder…
you're becoming Michael Jordan through that pen!

Let the Wind Carry Your Hope

Be vibrant, be free and flow as you go:
let the wind carry your hope!
The time is now, and there is no telling
how far or how high you will go:
let the wind carry your hope.
Pure and precious is the seed that you sow,
cool and refreshing is the breeze that you blow;
to whom we are destined, we may never know,
but in light of the question, we surely must go:
let the wind carry your hope!
Yes, this is the season to marvel our cause,
to show as the sun, to rest with the stars!
To where we are destined, we surely don't know,
but be vibrant, be free and flow as you go;
let the wind carry your hope!

In the Morning

Today's a new day; I finally made it through the night;
through the darkness and the gloom, through the wrong I found right!
I can't complain now; another day, I live to fight.
I can only appreciate this day and thank him for my life…
Just a few hours ago, I wondered if I would make it;
a heavy burden lay on my soul, and I feared that it would break it.
I doubted my circumstance and my will to overtake it,
I wearied a second chance, and my hope was no more favored…
But now that the morning come my eyes embrace the sun,
I see the beauty of all life now that the better night is gone.
The trees warmly embrace me, the birds sing me a song;
they praise the one above; his strength has made them strong!
In comfort, I now reflect; in great peace, do I move on.
I'm so happy that I held him as he kept me through the storm.
In the night, I considered my trial truly to be his test;
though at the time I felt he'd cursed me, now I see that I was blessed.
No more confusion, delusion, and hope tainted with fear
because, as a new day shines bright, so in the morning, all is clear!

I Smell Smoke

Do you see that smoke rising:
something is on fire;
either God is descending
or man has gone higher!
let us go investigate to see what they see,
we have heard from abroad
that the truth sets you free!
Their passion shines bright,
they must hold a true flame;
God must be among them,
God must have came!
For the excitement of their joy does create fire
until smoke must deploy by way of their true desire!
There must be something there, something made to inspire;
either God has descended, or man has come higher!

Love Makes Us Courageous

Like fungi spreads, as darkness caves us,
despair can be contagious!
Though acts of hate condemn our faith
love makes us courageous.
We deeply sigh a coward's cry
as the pains of life enslave us;
though some would quit, we can't forget
love makes us courageous!
We stand to fight; our battle cry
is said the song of ages.
If we should die, we gave our life
as love makes us courageous…
We burn our bread!
Behold the dead:
no such fate awaits us…
We don't die; we multiply
as love makes us courageous!
With no hope, some take their life,
erase their names from pages;
BOLD is the book for which we write
that love makes us courageous!

Seeing The Invisible

In the invisible, there is something I see
standing in front of 'what could've been'
and behind 'what could possibly be.'
What only time can tell
is made clearly known to me
when I consider the invisible
to be something I see!

The carnage of her car wreck
left the vehicle a mangled mess,
as bystanders approached
they suspected of her death,
but to everyone's surprise
she set up gradually;
seven months pregnant,
she stepped out casually…

"I-29 is shut down!"
the news station reported.

"Typical hit and run!"
the police retorted.

But as the fire truck and ambulance
pulled onto the scene
there stood the lady and her baby
with a look so serene…

"You should be dead right now!
Just take a look at your car;
you were in a head-on collision
and you don't have a SCAR!"

"I know…" she replied.
"But just as we left,
a coworker of mine
wanted to pray at my desk…"

In the invisible, there is something I see
standing in front of 'what could've been'
and behind 'what could possibly be.'
What only time can tell
is made clearly known to me
when I consider the invisible
to be something I see!

I Know Everything, and That's Why I'm Still Learning

A man that knows anything
knows that he knows nothing at all;
when I claim to know everything,
I'm saying that I know how to fall.
You see, my mind keeps changing like the world keeps turning;
just when I come to know everything,
that's when I choose to keep learning!

Some might think it arrogance to claim to know everything
but I'm not humbled by the ignorance of ordinary beings;
I'm chastened to intelligence by something more supreme,
I gravitate toward relevance in a world of worthless things…

My education is important;
in my mind, I'll never settle!
Lest I learn, lest I grow:
how shall I resist the devil?

Because a man that knows anything
knows that he knows nothing at all;
when I claim to know everything,
I'm saying that I know how to fall.
You see, my mind keeps changing like the world keeps turning:
just when I come to know everything,
that's when I choose to keep learning!

You Are the Exception

The ability to choose lies solely with you!
You are the exception; this is the truth!
How great do you want to be:
how special, how new?
Whatever you want to be
will not become an excuse…
You are the master of it all;
how much influence do you wish to have?
How different do you dare to be:
how good or how bad?
You can shape the world around you,
you are the norm of society:
don't let your cry be smothered,
don't let your calling be covered,
never trade your vision for the views of another.
Stand out, don't blend in,
let them tell you apart;
shine bright, be bold
with the hope of your heart!
You are the solution to the problem,
the outcome is your lesson;
teach the world to know your name:
you are the exception!
There has never been anything like you
nor will there ever be!
So be yourself;
no matter what they call you,
always be free!

Keep them guessing at their charts,
don't let them pin you down to the system;
make a fool out of the wise
and baffle this world's wisdom!
Keep chasing after your heart!
If you can 'choose' you are destined
to be greater than they thought...
YOU ARE the EXCEPTION!

By Means Of Many Wonders

By means of many wonders
will we finally follow God.
He leads us into the unknown
using his staff and his rod.
To follow him takes courage
as he is proving our heart;
with great signs and many wonders
we find the path that he charts.
He leads us out with all his glory
to a place we are ashamed;
naked and vulnerable,
a place where only he can save.
In our hour of desperation
he reveals to us his wonders;
when we are made to question,
that's when our questions are uncovered.
We discover that our possibilities
exist solely with him;
when we come upon the impossible
we find that he is our only friend.
Though great fear grip us
in sight of what we can't see,
we are assured of his existence
as the truth sets us free.
Yes, the truth can be blinding:
we walk by faith through the night
all to find that our doubts are wonders,
for our future is bright!

Our Future Forever

How we coexist today could be our future forever,
our relationships exemplify a grand scheme so clever:
who'd have thought that the way we are now
could be our future forever?
That person cut you deep,
they caused you much pain,
however, to forgive them would be cheap
when you look from long range.
Just weigh their life in the balance,
consider the way it shapes you.
Does knowing that they exist
build you, or does it break you?
See, if that person exists forever, then in a sense, it creates you.
Truly, if you deny that that person exists, then in a sense, it negates you.
Suddenly, I see with clarity the golden rule:
love your neighbor as yourself;
treat others how you want them to treat you.
We are defined by one another;
by one another, we get better;
our relationships exemplify a grand scheme so clever.
The only way to ensure our future
is to ensure our future together.
Yeah, that person cut you deep!
Will you forgive them: probably never...?
But consider...
the way that we are today could be our future together,
therefore,
we must fix relationships now for our future forever!

I Have an idea

There is something more valuable than a car or a house:
than a business, than a job, than a child or a spouse.

I have an idea...

I have something more to be desired
than anything you can see;
something that lies within me,
something that sets me free!

I have an idea...

This thing can change the course of history,
can alter reality and time,
can shed light in the darkest places,
can bring hope to a troubled mind...

I have an idea...

I have a weapon so destructive to the very foundations of death
that those without this weapon feel as though they have nothing left!

I have an idea...

I Write Poetry That Makes Me Afraid to Write more

The feeling-after is the same as the feeling-before;
I write poetry that makes me afraid to write more…
There's a voice in my head saying, "You don't have what it takes!
There's nothing real about you; all your words are fake!"
But from the time my pencil hits the page, I begin to create
a poem that shocks me as my reality shakes!
The words flow out with rhythm like the beat of a drum,
the tone comes from my soul like the sound of a hum.
I stop in midsentence to read the work that I've done,
and inspired by each sentence, more ideas speedily come.
Suddenly, another voice appears and courageously shouts:
his timing so graceful, his word choice so tasteful,
he pours out my heart to me as my pencil is moving hasteful;
covering every question, refreshing me on each lesson
until my mind, body and soul are rested instead of restless.

As I come to a close, I look up in amazement,
reflecting on the words now filling these pages.
Everything is so right; I don't want to put anything wrong
lest I tarnish a good word or ruin a perfect song.
Now my heart is no longer heavy and the fear is all gone;
but in reverence of what I've written, the fear is still strong.
The voice of doubt drowned out; his words make me sure.
Through this poetry, he's showing me my heart is still pure:
healing me from within while providing me with the cure.
The feeling-after is the same as the feeling-before;
I write poetry that makes me afraid to write more…

Pleasure Beyond Comprehension

We may never fully understand what God wants;
what he wants is beyond our comprehension.
No, we cannot know the heart of God or put a value on our lives
because what his heart desires has no limits!
He is ruled by his emotion, governed by a holy spirit;
there's no telling how far he'll go. The truth is that we'll never know
the purpose of his decisions nor the reason for our existence.
He has established us to an end that we may never uncover,
created us to a cause we'll never fully discover.
Who can be the judge of what God deems right;
who can see the love of a passion so bright?
Why were we created; what is the meaning of life?
Whatever pleasure God has is evading of sight…
To what ends he has made us, for what reasons he's shaped us
may be the tools that build us or the skillful hands that break us…
To know what truly pleases God, to find the heart of his decisions
is to be captive of a pleasure that goes beyond our comprehension!

My World

My world is as big or as small as I
chose it to be.
At times people stare and wonder
looking at me.
At times I blank out, staring as if there's
something I see.
But it's my world, and it's as big or as small as I
choose it to be...

At times I feel trapped
inside another dimension,
I can't go back to my ignorance,
I must live with decisions.
I can't go back to care-free,
I must carry convictions...
I must face all that I see
through the world I've envisioned!

At times, although I'm present,
people can tell that I'm somewhere else:
looking inside my heart
as if seeing it for myself...
Because what you see
and what I see
may not always be
eye to eye
sometimes there's a higher calling
of which our vision must comply...

You'll find me blanked out from time to time
staring dead at the ground
as if there's something there,
as if there's something I've found.
You might catch me in a gaze looking amazed:
eyes wide open staring at food trays...
Showing concern, you might take a glance
to see what I see,
confused you might return:
it's not you, but it's me...
I'm in another dimension
somewhere in the galaxy,
because it's my world,
and it's as big or as small as I
choose it to be...

The Strength of The Truth
Is the Arm of The Lord

What's more fatal than a gun?
What's more deadly than a sword?
What's more powerful than the truth,
which is the arm of the Lord?

Please don't mistake his kindness for weakness;
I assure you that the truth is not weak…
The arm of the Lord is still strong
and the truth is still deep!

There are worse things,
there is something more scary
than a militia with weaponry
or an advanced military…

If those guns aren't aimed for justice,
if those weapons aren't meant for peace,
there may be repercussions;
you may be in for a treat…

The arm of the Lord is still strong,
the truth is heavy and deep!
More powerful than any weapon
is the end that we meet…

The Great Part About the Gospel

The great part about The Gospel is
its revealing of the truth!
With elated eyes, do we enquire
of this everlasting proof!
It is the story of our redemption,
it is the glory of all our pain,
it is the confidence of our soul,
it is the keeper of our name.

Within The Gospel,
indeed, there is a great part,
even the story of our lord and savior, Jesus
who stole away our hearts!
Showing us the way to salvation;
through his pain, we are free!
The great part about The Gospel
is the great part about you and me.

This story of which we hold
so dearly in our hearts
is a lamp unto our feet
and our light into the dark!
Without it, we would be lost,
without it, we'd live in fear;
without instruction to the-way,
without direction, we'd disappear…

The great part about The Gospel,
the great part about what we preach
is the message of salvation
to all that it may reach!

Let Things Go as They Should

Lord, I'd be a fool to mistake your kindness for weakness,
so, please humble this man to understand meekness.
That you've got a job to do in bringing justice back to earth;
so many, cry to you, and it's time that they know their worth...

It's only fair that they finally know how much you care;
that you would level cities for them in seconds,
that your throne is not a chair...

Who am I to object, proclaiming my false sense of peace,
indulging in a world that solely benefits me...?

Lord, I'd be a fool to mistake your kindness for weakness;
now, who am I to be a fool,
to turn a blind eye to their suffering,
to let injustice rule?
If they have had it bad in this life,
in which, I have had it good
then let the tables turn, oh Lord,
let things go as they should.

Curse Breaker

The weight of all my ancestors' rests upon my shoulders…
Now, with the strength of ten men, I break curses and lift boulders!
I am the chosen-one of my lineage; the buck stops with me.
I will undo the sins of my past as my seed I set free!

I am a curse breaker…

Generation after generation, and I was born for such a time as this!
I was brought into this world to kill the evils that exist!
I have not only put an end to every lie in my family tree,
but I have even enlarged my family that every lie have fear of me!

I am a curse breaker!

A Dead-Letter

These words have life!

They are living breathing inspiration;
ideals from a mind full of creation;
instructions to ambition, guidelines to motivation;
pep talks for people void of aspiration!

These words have life!

These words have weight, like gravitation!
These words have a presence in this world;
these words demand appreciation.
These words are alive: as though a person living inside a book
who holds up a mirror to all that dare to look.
These words are living caring, sharing, and giving;
understanding of our heart while at the same time convicting.
These words so prudently put reassure us that things get better!
When will they die: probably never...
For though in a book, they're still alive;
not just a dead-letter!

Jealousy Is a Powerful Motivator

It will take you to extremes
and redefine your dreams
when you look at what you've lost
and finally, see what can't be seen…
The hardest part, you will discover,
is coping with a lover
who took their love away from you
only to give it to another…

Only then do we find strength and willpower to fight!
Only then are we grateful convinced on doing what's right!

When we see from where we're stranded
and realize that we took for granted
something we truly loved
it changes the circumstances…

Our excuses have proven useless,
now we treasure the second chances;
we value the thing we lost
to the level that it advances!

Just knowing that if you won't
there's someone that will,
produces in us a power
based upon what we feel…

Of all our emotions,
one is the greatest activator!
Yes, even jealousy
is a powerful motivator!

There Is Power in The Truth

The truth is powerful,
there is power in the truth!
By it, chains are broken;
by it, bonds are loosed;
by it, we are bound
subjects from our youth;
held captive to its glory
yet enquiring of its proof;
testing all of its strength,
while seeking out its use,
all to find…
The truth is powerful
and there is power in the truth!

At times, we are led astray,
subtly putting the truth away;
in denial of its presence,
in dread of its dawning day.
But as gravity to what-matters,
as the worlds revolve the sun,
we cannot pull ourselves away
from the way that we've begun!
Our story is to its glory,
our destiny will not subdue;
the truth is much too powerful,
there is power in the truth!

So, as birds that take flight,
we are made free in its plight:
learning from our mistakes,
embracing our wrong from our right.
There are no cages that can contain us
nor chains that may refrain us,
for in the power that we possess,
while transforming, it does change us.
Incinerating a shallow shell
while liberating a heart of proof;
we find the truth can be very powerful
but we are powerful in the truth!

God Will Make a Way

All hope is not in you; don't worry, it's okay...
Your butt is covered by his plan;
just know... God will make a way.

Sometimes we fall short; sometimes we fail the mission,
that doesn't mean it's all over; that doesn't change God's vision...
With God, nothing is wasted; even our accidents come into play.
Everything serves its purpose so take it day by day...
He'll make a beauty of our messes, a masterpiece with our mistakes;
he'll turn evil into good; he'll amaze you with his grace!
In the midst of all our turmoil, it seems our suffering will stay
but beyond our drawn conclusion is the creation of his way!
There's something good in the distance;
by faith, we will witness something great!
No, all hope is not in you; don't worry, it's okay...
Your butt is covered by his plan;
just know... God will make a way.

But first, You Must Believe

Truly, anything is possible!
No, things are not what they seem,
but this very world is a fabrication
of all who dare to dream!
Why should you settle for this mediocrity
when inside you lives a king;
struggling with oppression and depression
when you're a supernatural being?
Every day you hear it calling you:
that 'something greater than what you are.'
As the grumblings of a stomach,
you hear your guts as though they starve!
Just admit that you're empty,
why pretend to be content?
Confess that you're unhappy;
to change your heart, you must repent...

This is the start of something greater,
when one looks beyond the things he sees
to discover the impossible
and fulfill his wildest dreams!
Just imagine all that power
lying at your fingertips...
You can shape your very world,
your very world is limitless...
Without a dream, you have NOTHING;
no, things are not what they seem...
truly anything is possible
but first, you must believe...

Just By Faith

I can turn the world around
just by faith!
I can change my life today
just by faith!
My faith makes me right,
I'm made right by faith,
made fair because I believe
that I have what it takes...

What is good for the world?
What is right for the times?
What is fair for the people?
What is true to the mind?

The just shall live by faith;
by faith, justice is kept alive!

Yes, just by faith
is their faith justified!

I'm right because I believe that
right is on its way:

if you ask me how I know,
I'll say, just by faith!

I can turn the world around,
I can change my life today;

my hope is good enough,
and I have every right to say...

I'm right because I believe I'm right:
I'm Just by Faith!

You may not see it here today
but I believe it's on its way...

These hypocritical mockers
seek to steal my peace away!
They want to trap me in their lie
that all is not okay.
If that is their belief,
let them believe the things they say,
but as for me, I perceive
there's a difference every day.

I can turn the world around!
I can change my life today!

I don't know how it works
but 'works' is not the way!

If you ask me how I know
I'll say, just by faith!

For Every Circle, There's A Square

For every circle, there's a square:
someone who truly cares,
someone that you can trust,
someone who's always fair.
Often known as the runt,
often taking the jokes brunt,
the one everybody teases:
they use him to make fun.
He's so serious, so real
that it's funny to take him lightly.
He works hard, stays humble
and handles people politely.
Although everybody laughs
at every one of his mistakes,
he's at the center of their circle
because he's what makes them great!
Cause when you're down to the wire
and all the fake friends are gone,
you need at least one in your circle
you can truly depend on.

Though many take him as a joke,
you look to him to keep it real!
And when you're afraid of what others will say,
you know he'll relate to how you feel...
Because everybody needs:
someone who truly cares,
someone that they can trust,

someone who's always fair.
Though you're the brunt of every joke,
you're the truth of every dare!
They are grateful just to know you,
they know they're holding something rare…
Though they treat you as the worst,
keep treating everybody fair!
For every wrong, there is a right,
for every circle, there's a square…

Shining in the dark

Amongst the doom and the gloom, you'll find this fire a spark:
just a flicker of perfection shining in the dark!
In a world that breeds chaos, where corruption pleads its pain,
is something that stands alone; in the darkness, it seems strange.
Its light is captivating; for what reason does it shine,
seeing the darkness surrounding it desires to make it blind?
Amongst the doom and the gloom, amongst the wicked do we find
one whose heart is still pure, and in the darkness, it shines.
Reflecting light from the heavens, at night it stands amongst the stars;
intrigued by its presence, we marvel to know its cause.
Could something of great value lie wait in the dirt?
What is the purpose of such shining upon the face of the earth?
We draw closer to such a sight to uncover its worth,
seeing that it is pure though it is covered in dirt.
Amidst the chaos and corruption is one retaining their hope;
amongst the turmoil of soil is the roar of such glow!
It must be precious, we hope; it must be diamonds or gold,
for it has beauty-of-heart amongst the darkest of souls.
Though it shines in the day, in the night, it shines most.
Though besieged by evil, it holds true to its post.
It has piqued our curiosity with hopes to capture our heart,
for it is rare in our sight when we find what was lost.
Amongst the doom and the gloom is this fire a spark:
just a flicker of perfection
shining in the dark!

Get knocked Down: Stand Back Up!

Get knocked down: stand back up!
Stand to your feet: get up, get up!
Positivity won't leave you; you were born with the fight!
Do your victory dance; you were born with the hype!
You feel physically beaten, ragged, and torn,
but the spirit won't leave you; shake it off and keep going!
Some are betting against you, and some are in favor;
you've been undefeated so long, don't let your confidence waver.
You got here on your own, so don't let anyone make you!
See, right here at this moment, you are the maker;
the beginning and the end, the alpha and the omega!
Own this very moment as the author and creator!
What they will say about you if you stumble and fall
is nothing compared to what they'll say if you don't get up at all…
The reporters may report it, but you are the writing the story,
so take a deep breath and seize your moment of glory!
Stand back to your feet and step back into the fire;
life's not done with you yet; show this world you're a fighter!
Go out with a blaze of glory, in a blaze of glory burn UP,
because life will knock you down, but you can choose to stand up…

My Story the Talk of The Town

I stand up just to fall down,
look up when no one's around;
my story, the talk of the town,
a friend nowhere to be found…

If angels have wings, then they fly,
but devils go down as they die.
If you know of the pain when you cry,
what sense is there wondering why?

So, I fall down just to stand up,
and when no one's around, I look up;
my life, proceeding the ground,
my story, the talk of the town.

I envision myself as a king,
make-marry like wedding bells ring;
if angels have songs, then they sing
but devils have sorrow they cling.

I can if I will, so I must
arise from the ashes and dust;
take hold of this glorious crown,
if they stare, I shall not look down.
For I fall down just to stand up
and when no one's around, I look up;
my life, proceeding the ground,
my story, the talk of the town…

Born from Necessity

What are the makings of greatness
but the soul of one with the recipe!
For that fire in the belly and a grumbling stomach,
they are born of necessity!

Comfort and ease cripple desire
and are the death of innovation,
but heartache and trouble fan the fire
that burns in desperation!

Wherever we find the greatest need,
there we shall find the greatest good;
wherever we find that there is no need for change,
death does lurk, as it should...
Time and time again, we see beauty spring from adversity
to let us know that we cannot grow without a sense of urgency.

What are the makings of greatness, you ask...?
What shapes creatures of such complexity?
As sure as the sparks fly upward,
as sure as the deep has destiny;
the sorrows and pains of this life adjourn
that they are born from necessity!

The Darkest Paths Are Preserved for The Brightest Lights

Show me someone special, someone precious,
someone distinct from all the rest;
I'll show you someone unmistakable and unbreakable,
procuring life from death.

The blackness of the path that stands before you,
the evil of the path you left behind
is the reason why the world adores you,
is the cause for which you shine!

You may suffer a great deal,
you may weary the time spent,
but the shadow of death is cast upon
the life to which it's lent.

So, should this world grow colder,
should evil have its night,
fret not the path of which you chose,
but behold your soul ignite!
For the darkest paths are preserved for
those who have the brightest light.
You will always have the strength you need
even before the fight...

Have you always had it hard and tough,
or has life for you been easy?
Rest assured that you have had enough
of whatever you have needed.

Be not fearful of what lies ahead,
for he has prepared you all your life!
Even when you were unaware
he knew the path you'd light...

So, shine bright into the night as though the dark excites your flame!

Shine bright into the night as though your pleasure prescribes your pain!

Shine bright into the night; force the world to change.
Clear a path into the unknown for all the world to gaze!

The Strength I Need
from Day to Day

Each heart knows its own bitterness,
and no one else can fully share its joy.
You see me standing strong today,
but you don't know how I'm destroyed.
You don't realize with your eyes
the salty tears my soul cries,
and you don't understand what it takes to stand
when your soul is crushed from the inside.

Only God knows what I've been through,
only God knows to this day
the strength I need for every hour,
the importance each time I pray.

Only God knows my tender heart,
only God sees my wounded scars
Though you be blind, my peace of mind
is that God tells us apart…

For if he saw me the same as you,
never knowing when something's wrong,
then cursed would be my wretched soul;
I'd sing no brand-new song…

Comfort Ye

Sometimes good people refuse to be comforted
as if the vexing of their soul is justifiable punishment.
And the demons will find a home wherever a man will
should he be bound to their desires to divide, steal, and to kill.

Should the devil get you alone, he'd even pit you against yourself,
divided you, and break you down till it's bad for your mental health.
So, when you're up against life's trials when storm clouds are arising,
even if it's your fault, with a steady hand, he guides us…
Let go of the guilt, of your pain, break free; hear his gentle voice calling,
"Comfort ye… comfort ye…
Even in the worst times, I got your back; you're with me!
Let not your soul be vexed: comfort ye… comfort ye…."

Pain has a tendency to stick to the soul,
remind you of your regret till you're afraid to let go,
but as water is to a river, in his love, let it flow!
If it weren't a part of the grand plan, then it wouldn't be so…

Please take me by the hand; I refuse to let go.
I promise I'll understand even if you're standing is low…
Don't let your head hang; lift up your eyes, and you'll see
there is a gentle voice calling, "comfort ye, comfort ye…

Even in the worst times, I got your back; you're with me!
Let not your soul be vexed: comfort ye… comfort ye…."

It's Empowering to Empower You

⁓⚬⚭⚬⁓

I'm glad that I could assist you;
happy to fill your heart with Joy.
By no means is heaven emptied
when angels from God deploy.
It is my pleasure and my honor
to satisfy your soul.
Indeed, the spirit of God does fill me
as I use it to make you whole!
My fire is not consuming,
turn aside to see this burning bush.
It is warming and reassuring;
it will give you just the push!
There are others who seek your soul
with a desire that will devour you
but the passion I've found is pure;
it is empowering to empower you!

I need not money for what I love
because I do what sets me free;
to see your spirit happy
does elate the soul of me!
Finally, I have discovered
the one thing I can do forever.
I will not weary of this task,
but each day, I will be better!

Therefore, I am happy I could assist you;
Glad I am able to fill your heart with joy.
By no means is heaven emptied
when angels from God deploy.
This gift: it keeps on giving;
never shall it sour you,
but as the sweetness of my soul,
it is empowering to empower you!

I Gotta Keep Writing

This world is squeezing me dry!
All I can do is try
to push out a poem
for the sake of knowing
I still know how to fly:
To break free from my mind
which is enslaved to the world's whimsical way of thinking;
to break free from the chains, break free from the sound of their clinking…
Poetry is my portal
by which I travel to distant lands
grasping for eternity
while counting the grains of sand…
I gotta keep writing.

Where The Finest Are Made

My heavenly father only wants the best for me,
and so, for greatness, he has shaped my destiny;
to be the cream of the crop, to be the best, he's tested me.
With only the hardest trials and longest miles, he's blessing me.
I now look toward my journey with great peace and harmony,
for he has forged me in the fire and beset me with armory.
He has made me sharp as a sword, made me to cut like a blade;
to discern good from evil, to be tempered, and to behave.
His disciplining of me was excruciating yet crucial;
heartaches and hard breaks, though painful, have proven useful!
At times, I look with envy toward those whose life has been easy;
at times, I question what he's destined and why so many must need me.
Although my position seem untimely, although my duty seem strange;
though my mission be impossible, my mind will not change.
He has purposed me for greatness in these perilous days
he is refining me in a furnace where the finest are made!

Till the Ground

Till the ground, oh God!
Oh Lord, break up that old foundation.
Plant new Hopes inside our hearts,
redefine a new creation.
Humble us, oh God, bring us back into our basement;
open up our hearts to submit unto your placement.
Give us renewed vision; let revelation be known.
Plant the truth deep within us; you have seeds to be sown.
Let these trials and tribulations uproot us and reshape us
Till the ground, oh God;
break up that old foundation.

We Can Save The World

No, not he can save the world;
no, not she can save the world;
no, not you can save the world;
no, not me can save the world:
but say it with me,
all together now…

"We can save the World!"

See, the problem with capitalism is the corruption that comes with it.
If you have the money by your side, why hold it? Why not give it?
So many preach about love, but when are we going to live it?
With everyone out for self, the community's all gimmick!
We have problems in the home; we have issues at the heart;
it seems we need an intervention before the family falls apart.
Now, before we get into it, let me tell you from the start,
no one person here can do it, but if we all play our part…?

No, not he can save the world;
no, not she can save the world;
no, not you can save the world;
no, not me can save the world:
but say it with me,
all together now…

"We can save the World!"

The reality is, the world in which we live,
could easily become a better place,
because at the heart of us all is a seed so small:
it turns out a common ground, is all it takes...
If we are poor apart, then our mind is sharp
to see that together we are great!
The world needs love, so just a great-group-hug
could easily rectify all our faith!
So,
No, not he can save the world;
no, not she can save the world;
no, not you can save the world;
no, not me can save the world:
but say it with me,
all together now...

"We can save the World!"

Yes,
a superman can save the day, but that's a temporary fix;
it takes more than just a man to kill the evils that exist.

When we all choose a side in the callous of our pride
the one thing we have denied lies is in the midst!
A willful heart and open hands, with the courage that we can,
stands one at whom none can ball a fist.
He makes the message ever clear; salvation is ever near,
there is a way in which the world can still be fixed!
As perfect love cast out fear, there is a voice in every ear
persuading men to listen to their hearts.
Great minds think alike, against whom do you fight
when together we are better than apart...
So,
No, not he can save the world;
no, not she can save the world;

no, not you can save the world;
no, not me can save the world:
but say it with me,
all together now…

"We can save the World!"

A Powerful People

Why we don't agree with one another is purely deceitful
because if we could work together, we'd be a powerful people.

If we could celebrate our differences and use our strengths to our advantage
then we could conquer what divides us and secure a more stable planet.

Yes, you and I, we disagree, but for reasons we hope to see;
and it takes reason to understand that we both see hope equally...

One is a fighter, and one is much more passive:
now, please explain to me the dynamics of patience and passion:

the passion of Christ made him impatient,
but the patience of Christ made him passive.

He learned to celebrate the difference,
and to be one with his actions...

He moved as one man who holds the entire world in his body;
a rebel for the cause, a man for the Godly.

Proving that what divides us isn't greater than what brings us together,
he fought for something in the moment that would have implications forever...

The brilliance of his war highlights the glory of his fight
to prove to an entire world that great minds think alike,

that our disagreements with one another are purely deceitful;
that if we could work together, we'd be a powerful people...

Go with Them

When somebody leaves you, it's tempting to think them gone,
but their life has lessons that lead you along.
They may have left an impression; yes, you may never forget them
so that every day that you wake, you can't help but go with them.
So, go with them into the journey of life and learn from their struggle.
That's the only way that life can continue; that's the only way we can love
them.
Their spirit resides with us unto the ends of the world;
they are gone but not forgotten, as the passing of pearls.

For instance, if you had a bad breakup and there's a chance you'll never
make up,
there's still a chance that their life can still cause you to wake up.
No, they may never come back, and to them, you may be dead,
but don't let their purpose go to waste; cherish their life instead,
go with them.
Go with them into the future because in the past live the dead;
they only came into your future in hopes that you might think ahead
so, go with them.

When someone precious comes and goes,
it leaves our soul with scars and holes,
but in their life is held the lessons
and once they're gone, we must accept them
so, go with them.
Yes, go with them; embody their spirit outside of their body.
Go with them, just as Jesus came to make us more godly:

his struggle was real, and the pain of his life
was a lesson he taught for days of advice.

Yes, go with them, don't let their sacrifice be in vain.
They are gone but never forgotten, as long as the truth remains.

Go with them because it's the only way to forget them...

Yes, they may have left, but you did not lose
when you gain from their life and walk in their shoes.
Go with them...

Write Away the Pain

Write away the pain,
embrace the memory of your shame;
give life to what is dead,
put a pencil to your page!

The stories of old have yet to be written!
Our future be told, the truth was a witness
that under layers and layers of bitter resentment
we hid from our truth before it was written,
that the lies in our eyes can hardly give light,
that the fear of our tears is the reason we fight.
Now, the pain will remain, and pain will we like,
till we discover our heart through pain that we write...

So, write away the pain...

Pick up the pencil again,
wage war for holy ground;
all of heaven wants you to win!
As your thoughts freely flow
may armored angels descend
yielding sword and shield
for the victory of your pen!

We battle not with flesh and blood
but with the principle of the matter;
we wrestle with right and wrong
until spoils, we gather.

But as the pen bleed on the page,
we cleanse away the stain;
yes, as true as blood in the vein,
we write away the pain...
The pain of resentment, the pain of defeat,
the pain of regret, the pain of our grief
are all distant memories from the truth that we seek:
that we are right in every way when the truth we have reached...

For times you would explode,
for times you would blame,
for times that you would suffer in silence and shame;
the bitterness of the past, we are not meant to contain,
but they shall hear your cry at last,
when you write away the pain...

The Freedom of The Fall

Who'd have thought that there's something better than standing tall;
who'd have guessed that there's nothing more sure than when you fall:
when you let go of all and cast-off restraint,
not by your own will, but by the fact that you can't;
when your giving-in is, hardly, a gift of which you give free;
when your 'letting go' is a loss to the ends of which you can't see.
But this is a bizarre event; as if, something you cannot call,
because you can't predict the future nor the freedom of the fall.

Thank God life has curves, twists and turns indeed,
interactions and distractions from the hope on which we feed.
Sometimes, to stir our soul, we must know the depth of all its pain;
the root of all its cause; the reason we remain.
Such a stirring of the soul is to the ends we die,
and should we bring our life to question, we will know the reasons why.
No, we shall not be sure; no, we shall not be bold at all,
for in the knowledge of this truth is the freedom of the fall.

Our journey seems prolonged as, along dark roads, we stumble.
We can't outwit our failure, and we can't deride the humble.
To even know our fate is to know nothing at all
so that each step that we take ensures the freedom of the fall…

Embrace, I say, the pain,
hold fast unto the call…
the longer that is, the wait
the more free is the fall.

May you plummet to your ascension!
There's something greater than standing tall…
So, arise, oh mighty one, amidst the freedom of the fall!

The Things we Walk Through Yet Don't Know the Answer To

Oh, the things we walk through yet don't know the answer to

I just take it day by day; each step by faith.
Confronted with trial and challenges the likes of which
I, currently, cannot overcome, so I just wait for the light to switch…

Oh, the things we walk through yet don't know the answer to.

My blue skies fade to grey until the sun comes shining through.

See, I've been faced with situations where I didn't know what to do,
where the answer was beyond me,
like it was beyond me to see me through.

Oh, the things we walk through yet don't know the answer to.

At many days, I look behind and see a path, that at the time,
I couldn't see and was nowhere to find,
and what now is clear, at first, was blind…

Oh, the things we walk through yet don't know the answer to.

Many days I spent stuck; head no longer up;
at the end of my wit, only to land on my dumb luck…
I could never take the credit for what only God can do:
for the things I walk through yet don't know the answer to.

Daniel and the lion's den, suddenly, doesn't seem so long ago,
and neither do Shadrack Meshack and Abednego...

Standing before a fiery furnace, hands bound without a clue:
when they stepped out without a singe, I'm sure by then they knew...

But, oh, the things we walk through yet don't know the answer to.

Life

Life,
Although I cannot survive you,
your breath-taking display shall be the story I write to!
Just to be above ground, just to stand to my feet
is the grace of your glory, a love beyond me!

The majesty of your sky reveals the depth of your soul;
the countenance of your face is the truth to be told.
What I see inside of you is beyond what I can see;
but to feel your essence is the hope inside of me.

Life, you break me with gentle and loving hands;
life, you shape me with the mastery of your plan.
My eyes gaze intently at this most formidable foe
whose eyes pierce my heart and crown my head with lumps of coal.

I am but a baby before your power and might;
the innocence of infancy is the plea of my plight.
My arms too short to box with you,
yet you spar with me daily!
You nurture me to perfection;
for existence, you train me…

As a sensei, you advise me and then, silently, watch
as from my downfall to my rising you, graciously, plot.
In times that I am flustered by you, your cunning hands hold me.
In times I am undone, your crafty hands mold me.
Upon my heart, you write the story of the glory that sold me

as I behold the beauty of the truth, you have told me.
At times, you enrage me with a pain that enslaves me,
but only to ensure me that death cannot cage me!
Life, you are rather mean and rather nice,
rather tough but rather sweet,
rather free but rather priced!

Because the abundance of you no mortal-man can take,
you destroy this mortal-man for the glory of his fate!
Should I take you by the hand, you will lead me to my doom;
should I entrust you with my soul, you will spare me this cocoon.

Though I die for your reason, I fly as flowers bloom!
Should I surrender to your treatment; new life is coming soon!

Dream On Dreamer

Sprout wings and fly; break free your cocoon;
dream on, dreamer, new life is coming soon!
As soon as the sun sets, of such glorious display,
so shall the sun rise at the dawn of another day!
The magnificence of your design comforts a brilliant mind,
and true beauty never fades, but dazzling does it shine
Amidst the chaos and corruption is the will of the soul;
clamoring in the darkness is your luminous glow!
Your light is a hope, a prosperous breach;
your faith is a dream in the deepness of sleep.
As you awake, be unashamed, stand to your feet;
there is a message to proclaim a word you must speak.
Yes, like an angel from heaven descend like a dove;
bring hope to this world, bring peace from above!
Let your revelation be the occasion for your story of glory;
your inspiration: destination, towards which you move forward.
From the chains of deep darkness, you have rescued your soul;
now, let your spirit run free for the world to behold!
Should it gaze upon your essence and discern your demeanor,
it will shake at your perceptions; it will move at your finger.
For should it sleep upon a dream much evil shall linger,
but God forbid that you should sleep,
so, dream on, dreamer!

CHAPTER 4

Black Man

The First Born of The World

The darkness of his presence was the beginning of something great!

When darkness was upon the face of the deep;

upon the deep, was the darkest face…

The creation of such a one fearfully and wonderfully made;

the firstborn of the world was the be beginning of something great!

He was called to life with splendor having majesty at his heart;

his eyes shined bright as light, although his face was dark.

To become a holy nation: a priestly kingdom was his part.

To rule and judge the world was his mission from the start.

His quest to conquer came with much travail; it took much labor and pain

to subdue the kingdoms of the world under the glory of his name!

For by God was he called that for justice he should reign

a holy nation forever; a priestly kingdom he'd proclaim!

Now, as firstborn of the world chosen for what is fair,

to do the will of God is his purpose should he dare…

How Did You Get Here?

You!
How did you get here?
You are supposed to be dead!
How did you come into being?
How is it you walk with your head?

I thought I had imprisoned you,
I thought I had chained your kind up and locked you away!
The genocide should have extinguished you;
how is it your still here today?

You have no place here;
no, you should not be alive!
Who allowed you to walk in **purpose**,
who gave you permission to **thrive**?

No, you are not welcome!
No, there is no sign on the door,
but surely no one expected you to come
nearly as far as before.

Please, get out of my presence!
The light of your being is disrupting my peace!
It kills me to know you're alive,
it irks me to hear of your speech.

The fact that you stand here unbroken:
mind, fully, intact;

The fact that you endured extermination
is, in itself, an unlawful act.

You take your seat at the table;
next to me, you pull up a chair.

The fact that I now must dine with you is a burden too heavy to bear:
that now I must get to know the one I have denied;
that now I must be sure of the truth I have spoiled.
I must hear of your horrific story;
of the fear, to which I have toiled.

For I thought you to be dead;
long ago, I marked your path.

How in this world you stand here alive today
is a question I dare not to ask…

All I know is that it's a miracle you made it,
that I'm even seeing the likes of your kind.
Now you stand here today and question me,
rendering my eyes to be blind

Before you, I thought I had understood,
I thought the truth to be gone for good.

But now you stand here in full view of us all,
shining the light where it should.

While as yet, I thought we discouraged you:
who encouraged you;
with what *might* did you fight?
For we submerged you in utter darkness;
how in the world did you see light?

The fact that you stand here today,
of a truth, it is simply amazing!

To my own shame, I look in dismay;
bamboozled, I stand here gazing!

I don't know rather to kill you and cover you up,
or rather to love, adore and embrace you.
Today the truth has reared its ugly head
and now I muster the courage to face you.

I am humbled now and insecure
because of your doom, I was sure.

I mean, who'd have guessed the truth would rise again someday
and stand back up for more...

The Glory of His People

Ever since their journey out of Egypt,
these people have been a barren tree:
waiting patiently for their season,
holding steady through all their **grief**.
Though they set out as conquerors
in the plight of their holy king,
though they troubled the whole land
with a supernatural being;
their day has still not come,
their battle continues on.
For they waged war against the world
in the day their arm was strong,
and not soon after waging war,
they left-off to use their strength:
they put their God away
and replaced him with a fake…
Now they face the world
with the entire world at stake;
looking for their savior,
wandering through a desert place.
Indeed, they have a story
of which there is no equal;
only time will tell
the glory of his people…

Just Check Your History

The plagues and epidemics that we as black people face today is really no mystery.
For our God warned us long ago;
we were foretold:
just check your history.

For a people who **bear** the **KNOWLEDGE** of the **ONE** *TRUE* **LIVING GOD**
it's no surprise we be convicted, although today it *seems* odd…

Long before we were captives, we were kings and queens;
long before this nightmare of disaster, we had goals and dreams…

The **light** of our **hope** was *God,* and he revealed to us these things;
he warned us ahead of time what disobedience brings…

Today the truth unfolds right before our very eyes,
but it's no mystery as to why; for certain, it's no surprise…
that we be foreigners in a land, bought and sold as slaves;
that we be destitute and deprived, number one in jail and aids;
that our land be pillaged, and our children slaughtered
all before the day is done…

Aloof of where we started, look how far from God we've come:

just check your history…

Soldiers On a Different Battlefield

Don't worry; I won't judge you, not by the sword that you yield,
but all I'll say is that true-heart is hard to truly kill…
I show respect because the real *will* recognize the real…
I can't forget we're both just soldiers on a different battlefield…

Where we're at the battles thick,
but neither of us can seem to face defeat,
so you fight on my brother;
I pray the Lord your soul to keep.
From my youth was I taught
to know wrong from right,
and from your youth, it's true;
every day, you had to fight…

Don't worry; I won't judge you by the sword that you yield,
but all I'll say is that we were sold a different set of skills.
I show respect because the real *will* recognize the real.
I can't forget we're both just soldiers on a different battlefield…

Where you grew up, the war was brutal, and there lay many slain;
early on, you sought protection, and so you joined a gang…
From day one, I had protection, so I don't feel your pain…
and when you say that you had to do it: I'm sorry, but I don't share your shame…

With no clue as to who you were, you fought for life;
just to gain the time to train your mind to *know* wrong from right…
See, the *streets* was your father,

and you had *pain* for a mother;
now the scars that you bear
is like the blood between brothers…

"Show *no love*," they said,
"Because *love* will get you killed…."
It seems there's one way out of this game
after all the blood you've spilled…

Don't worry, I understand, and by no means will I judge!
When you give me that mean mug, I'll just take it as *mad-love!*
I've never seen the things you saw, so how could I understand your sight…?
From my youth, was I taught to know wrong from right,
but your heart has grown cold from all the boys that lost their life;
all the brothers that died in battle and all the foes that *paid the price;*
fighting valiantly in a war that has yet to be proclaimed,
on a field where the **honorable** are *still* to be ashamed…

You live your life on the edge now; it seems death is always at your door.
I know you wonder if it's worth it, if you should fight for something more.

I can't relate to you, my brother, but my **word** is as strong as steel!
God knows I will not judge you; not by the sword you yield…
but all I'll say is that ***True Heart*** is **HARD** to *truly kill…*
I show respect because the real *will* recognize the real…
I can't forget we're both just soldiers on a *different* battlefield…

Jordans In Jail

Locked-up potential is a **total waste** of **time**...
life is precious; coincidentally, so is the value of a mind.
See, at the souls of our feet is our purpose and design
to travel the earth's surface to whatever peace we find.
Will we find rest for our soul as the galaxies align?
Will our soul rest in peace knowing the value of our time?
Ashamedly I say, so many lives waste away,
so many minds are locked up,
so many feet are made to *stay*...
So, rather soaring in slow motion or stuck stale in a cell,
our potential needs focus: you ain't heard??
It's Jordans in jail!

Throughout life, we had coaches who had dreams we'd assail
who invested thousands into our bodies just to put thousands on bail.
They never imagined that our mind wasn't prepped to excel,
that our interior design was at Foot Locker for sale...
Getcha mind, bruh! The industry has manufactured your 'fail!'

Time is money, bruh! You ain't heard?

They got Jordans in jail!

So many had the opportunity but squandered their talent;
their gift came from above, but their ground was imbalanced.
When are we gonna learn that our knowledge is power,
see the beauty of our shoes as a withering flower…

Put the money on his books now, and later on, he'll prevail;
get your head in the books now, even if it's not in style:
it's not about looks!
Don't wait until you're headed to the jail to get 'booked'!

You should see the prison population:
their stats would leave you **shook**
their highlights would ***cross you over,***
oh, their stories would ***make you look…***

Now, you can't judge a book by its cover so, by the *cover*, I can't tell,
but I encourage you: define who you are **NOW**
cause', dog,
it's Jordans in jail!

Always Be Brothers

If it comes down to it, I know you got my back!
We are bound by blood, not just because we're black...
Word is 'we don't get along,' but this is not a fact;
we've just been through so much together that *we don't know how to act.*
Now, memories I've kept, though we go our separate ways.
I can't forget from where I come, nor the start-up of my days.
You were my first friend; we took baths with one another.
Only God knew it then, but *we'd always be brothers!*

All pride aside, I wore those hand-me-downs with pride;
and if a shirt was too big, I'd just tuck it inside.
And if we're just being honest, I appreciate your life
because even though we'd box, you still taught me how to fight.
I guess iron sharpens iron, and now, as men, we see
that it's **us against the world,** not **you against me!**

Now, we are bound by blood, not just because we're black...
So, if it comes down to it, you know I got your back.
Word is 'we don't get along,' but this is not a fact;
We've just been through so much together that *we don't know how to act.*
Truly God knew it then that we'd *need* each other,
that, even as *men*, we would always be *brothers.*

Let Me Through

I have somewhere I have to go,
I have something I have to do,
so, please,
let me through...

You are excused, now excuse me too
and please...
let me through...

You may pretend to be unaware,
but deep down, you always knew
that I was destined for greatness,
for a purpose that's bigger than you,
so please,
let me through...

Please don't stand in my way,
don't stand in the gap,
but step to the side
with those who clap
and please,
let me through...

The purpose I serve
should both of us fear;
please humble yourself
and respect why I'm here,
yes, please,
let me through...

My time is essential
I'm not here by mistake
so, spare me the time
and move out of the way
Yes, please,
let me through…

I should not have to tell you,
'This time, it's my turn.'
I've been ever so patient,
I've watched, and I've learned,
now please,
let me through…

I ask your permission,
I ask in advance
for you to be gracious
and give me this chance.
Yes, please,
let me through…

To what I aspire, we never shall know
lest I be pardoned the path which I go
So please,
let me through.

For many years now
I've been bound with these chains,
yet I am not bitter
but hope still remains.
So please,
let me through…

I have repaid my debt,
my time is complete.
I have learned my lesson
in taking my seat,

now please,
let me through…

I know this is different,
I know this is new,
that I should have freedom
and be just as you,
but please,
let me through…

You're Gonna Prove Em' All Wrong

There's something different about you,
something they never saw coming;
they said you wouldn't beat the odds
so, you hit the ground running!
Set apart from the start,
you could never 'just go along';
you put the pressure on your peers:
you're gonna prove em' ALL wrong…
Statistically speaking,
they thought by now you'd be done,
either dead or in jail,
but look at what you've become!
Now their eyes are wide open
to see the race you will run,
to see the distance you'll go,
now, they don't watch you for fun…
but now they're serious; they're curious
of what you could be;
your numbers are off of the charts,
you're like nothing they've seen!
Statistically speaking,
you'd be a fool to go on…
but off of the record,
you're gonna prove em' ALL wrong!
Blind with ambition
you set out on a futile mission;
with no regard for the standard,
they declared you dumb and ignorant.

But now your hope is a light
made to captivate minds;
set apart from the start,
it's your purpose to SHINE!
Now, they don't dare to compare you,
no, not by numbers alone!
Now they swear that you're rare,
but you won't last for long…
Statistically speaking,
you'd be a fool to go on…
but off of the record,
you're gonna prove em' ALL wrong!

Jesus Lifted the Ghetto with All the Strength of His Soul

—————————— ✦ ——————————

Jesus lifted the ghetto with all the strength of his *soul!*
Without a dollar to his name, he made the **whole world** *whole!*
Many starve and die in this world of corruption and pain;
and with all the strength in their soul, they call on his name.
They try to find a means of living while it only gets worse,
but only Jesus can do the job of lifting this curse...
Poverty-stricken and diseased, their bodies lie waste;
because, for the money and not God, they are moving with haste.
Those who gain the strength of God sell out for a chain,
and those blessed to survive just cause the world more pain.
Consequently, an endless cycle of destruction and strain
fills death's belly and inspires the grave!
This life is truly death; in this world, only the dead rest!
For the corruption of our soul is the taint of success
as the destruction of our flesh is the pain of progress
That's why…
Jesus lifted the ghetto with all the strength of his *soul!*

Hard Work Builds Character

Momma, *on crack!*
Daddy, gone; *no looking back!*
Living in the projects, not content with where he's at…

Now, to live life without purpose; nothing is scarier
than to die beneath the surface,
but *hard work… builds character…*

Crack-rock in his sock; on the corner he stands.
Cold gun on his waist; what a glorious plan!
They say the good die young; I guess it wasn't his time,
cause' she was seven months pregnant when he sold her a dime…
He was only 17 when he made up his mind
that he'd rather be a criminal devoted to crime
than to live his life soulless devoid of his shine…

He figured…
"Mannnn,
to live life without purpose, nothing is scarier
than to die beneath the surface,
but this hard-work builds *charactaaaa!"*

Now, that lifestyle was short-lived, but his guts would not give,
so, he kept grinding and kept hustling till the day came when it all did!
He sold dope to an undercover to soon later discover
that his house got shot up, bullets went through his younger brother…
Now he's staring up at the judge, eyes flooded with tears;
no reason for what he's done, no purpose to who he is…

The judge stares back with a sense of hysteria and says...
"Son,
to live life without purpose; nothing is scarier
than to die beneath the surface,
but hard work builds character...."

Now, the judge brought down the hammer, and he was the nail.
He was sentenced to 10 years when they threw him in jail!
'My, my,' how time flies; there's no fire where 'wind' dies.
He spent a decade in the joint; now, it's a new world through new eyes.
Now, life's hard, but he's grateful; they're living' large, but he's faithful!
He knows now that, to survive, his heart can't become hateful,
so, he goes to the local church and gives his life to the Lord,
gets involved with the work as a mentor for younger boys.
"Everyone, have a seat," he says as the kids entered the room.
"we've got material to cover, I know summer is coming soon."
Now, just as soon as they all sat down, one hand went up.
"Excuse me sir, but this class, *it sucks!*"
The teacher said, "boy be quiet," as he wrote with chalk.
"Learn some facts, and after class, we'll talk!"
Now, just as soon as the bell rang and all the kids got up,
the teacher turned to the boy and said, "talk to me, son; what's up?"
To see no one was looking, the boy looked back
and said, "when I was born, my mom did a crack,
and since my daddy's gone, I'm bout' to grab this pack."
Now, the teacher grabbed the boy's chair and pulled it close,
nearly breaking his Barrier
looked him square in the eyes and said,
"Son,
to live life without purpose, nothing is scarier...
than to die beneath the surface,
but ***hard work builds character...***

The Gangster in Him Had To, The Saint in Him Was Sad To

I won't forget the day a good friend persecuted me.
Peer pressure: gave into the man he used to be.
No doubt he had regrets, cried tears you'll never see
cause' way before he was a saint, he swore he'd always be a *G!*
Now, life choices stick around way longer than a tattoo;
if he could go back, don't cha know that he'd be *glad to.*
Many bad things that he did; the saint in him was sad to,
but he couldn't shed a tear because the gangster in him had to…

Let it blossom, let it fade away;
the innocent will see the beauty of another day!
In the ghetto, soldiers fade away,
and where mere boys took a stand, many men had fled away…
Now hard times make a hard heart sad too,
and good times to make a mad man glad too.
Now, no one knows how you let the streets grab *you:*
a real saint; church-boy, on the front pew!
I guess the 'school of hard knocks' is a fast school;
in the hood is where you learned to make fast moves…
and although the gangster in you had to,
the saint in you was sad too…
Under the weight of the world around you,
it's no wonder you stayed down with the same ones that downed you!
You didn't want to seem like a soft-flake,
and so, you played hard but never did wanna participate.
Selling crack: boy, you know the devil had you…

Pulling guns... I know the gangster in you had to,
but the saint in you was sad to...
Now, a man is just the sum of his decisions;
I'll write you letters; in the summer, pay you visits...
Pay no mind to the time, and how it's gone
because through six-inch glass, the love we had is *still strong!*
Rewind time, and we could never right wrongs,
but forgive and forget; that's how you live ya lifel*ong.*
Still, I gotta keep it real with cha, *G;*
I won't forget the day a good friend persecuted me.
Peer pressure: gave into the man he used to be.
No doubt he had regrets, cried tears you'll never see
cause' way before he was a saint, he swore he'd always be a G!
Now, life choices stick around way longer than a tattoo;
if he could go back, don't cha know that he'd be glad to:
many bad things that he did, yet he couldn't shed a tear...
and **I know** the gangster in him **had to**;
but STILL, the saint in him was *sad to...*

Lock Away Another Brilliant Mind

No, bars in chains can't contain the brain, so lock away another brilliant mind!

In a concrete jungle, he came up 'on the humble,'
and against all odds, he stayed out of trouble!
He was street and book smart, nothing like the others;
not given to violence but a 'lover of the brothers!'

Now, an educated black man is 'trouble a brew'…
Feared everywhere he went; yet, with him, it had nothing to do…

In a cold dark world, he couldn't help but shine;
holding all that power, it was just a matter of time
before a *hope* was discovered, and a *reason* they'd find…

after all…
bars in chains can't contain the brain, so lock away another brilliant mind.

Feared on every level, they threw him with the Mandellas,
the Martin Luther Kings, and all of the other rebels
to oppress, depress, and regress his shine;
to dim his light and to dull his mind…

Now, he picked up every book that his soul could find,
to break free the iron bars and the stones of lime;
even wrote his own book, in the course of time:
on a deserted island, the apostle John!

Revelations kept him going, of the truth that he knew;
that this world was not his home and that his days were a few...
that an educated black man was trouble-a-brew.
Feared everywhere he went; yet, with him, it had nothing to do...

See, he tried blending in but couldn't help but shine;
in a cold dark world, it's just a matter of time
before a *hope* is discovered, and a *reason* they find...
After all,
bars and chains can't contain the brain, so like away another brilliant mind...

When he finally got out, he was free indeed,
mind full of visions, full of hopes and dreams!
Now, he had no intentions of a plot or scheme,
but with honesty and faith, he still believed he could achieve...
Yet all too soon, he found himself out there alone;
reminded once again that this world was not his home.
He tried to find honest work, but a job he could never find.
It seemed like every application he signed was immediately declined;
like it was just the systems design...

Like, bars and chains can't contain the brain, so lock away another brilliant mind...

Somehow, he found a job within a major corporation,
but mopping hallway floors wasn't the final destination,
so he went back to school to be 'black with an education,'
got a job on the sales floor and rose to the occasion!
He broke every single record; and, to everyone's amazement, led the entire team in sales without a single standing ovation.

One day his boss called him in the office at nine;
pen and paper on the desk, in his chair he reclined...

"Our records found you're a felon; now you have to resign...
I'm sure that you knew that it was just a matter of time...."

125

Picking up the pen; on the paper, he signed
saying,

"I know…
bars and chains can't contain the brain,
so, lock away another brilliant mind…."

For Reasons, We Hope to See

We are oppressed and depressed in a land we are not free,
counted as sheep for the slaughter for reasons we hope to see...
Situations and circumstances where hope can never be
we are handed nonetheless for reasons we hope to see...
So, we dig deep, we try harder, we overcome, work smarter;
we dream away the horror to raise our sons and daughters.
No doubt this is a world where we are cursed to drop a seed,
no doubt this is a place where hope can never be,
yet we are placed in this place *for reasons we hope to see...*

The Wicked Will Vanish

Like inmates killed in incarceration,
the wicked will vanish…

Like slaves 'died' on a plantation,
the wicked will vanish.

Like the black young man shot down by the gunman,
the wicked will vanish!
Yes,
as the smoke from the black barrel clears,
without justice, without probable cause, they'll disappear:
the wicked will vanish!

As black babies stolen from a barren womb,
they will vanish;
as Christ's body 'stolen' from an opened tomb,
the wicked will vanish!

In A World Gone Mad Wanders a Madman Lost

In a world gone mad, wanders a madman lost;
no one to feel his pain, no one to weigh what it costs

to remain sane in a world that hasn't found what it lost,
to contain in one world all the rage of his thoughts…

His anger, oblivious to the world around him, he remains unseen;
suffering in his silence; a **nightmare of a dream!**

His truth is so disruptive that, just to *live*, he must die;
hiding behind closed doors, containing a lie…
For the happiness of others, he smothers his 'why';
suffocating his purpose, depriving his pride…

Have you ever seen a man carrying the weight of the world;
he is hardly at peace; his mind is in *peril!*

Those standing afar off, aloof of his pain,
would consider him a madman going **insane**;
a cold, heartless and cruel being void of affection;
a dark, angry, disturbed being vexed with depression…

But human eyes could never see the pain of his soul,
nor the weight of the world which, on his shoulder, he holds;
that in a world gone mad wanders a madman lost,
no one to feel his pain, no one to weigh what it costs

to remain sane in a world that hasn't found what it lost...
to contain in one world all the rage of his thoughts...

Those living carefree are at ease, for life is easy.
If you ask them, life is a breeze, but that's deceiving.
Because they don't understand what's on the other end of the spectrum;
they care nothing for the madman, hardly do they respect him...

They turn a blind eye to his pain for the sake of their peace;
now, blind is his rage when he *turn to a beast!*

Just another civilian of a civilization;
they cage him and chain him; of dignity, *rape him!*

To their judgment, he deserves it; that is the sum of their thoughts...

While as yet, he observes it; he weighs what it costs...
to remain sane in a world that hasn't found what it lost;
that in a world gone mad, wanders a madman *lost!*

I Just Bumped My Head on The Ceiling, and It Hurts!

Compare me to a giant; you're just mad because I thought of it first!
The truth is, I just bumped my head on the ceiling, and *it hurts...*

When the top isn't the top because someone has raised the roof
in a room full of pupils who *assumed* they were taught the truth...

there's a bit of indignation about the fact that we've come higher
than the intended expectation of the one tasked to inspire...

But if the fire fascinates them, I say let it burn;
there should be no limits to our knowledge, nor limits to what we learn...

Yes, compare me to a giant; fitting-in is the worst!
The truth is, I just bumped my head on the ceiling, and *it hurts!*

Please, don't put out my passion or quench my desire
to prevent a potential danger or to contain a wildfire...

I say, let the truth be told to men of low degree
who have been deprived of the truth; told that they could never *see;*

told they were inferior,
taught that they could never meet the expectation;
when on the interior,
they were the teacher's main frustration...

Now that there is one in the room who *truly* has raised the bar,
the one you never expected is now outshining the star...

The truth takes many forms, and some we resent to see;
yes, some would crush our pride while at the same time set us free!

No, I don't take offense to your good intension
because I know now that I am not the worst...
but compare me to a giant:
truly, I just bumped my head on the ceiling, and it hurts...

For bad-reason, you shut me down,
for good-reason, I raise the question...
Now, lest **we all** should learn,
you *withhold* a **lesson...**

I'll die of boredom in your classroom before I make it worse!
The truth is, I just bumped my head on the ceiling, and it hurts!

It hurts to know that the truth we will not show.
That my teacher withholds the truth is all the *truth* I know.

Never should you lower or limit the expectation;
that's like throwing a game for the sake of compensation...

No longer is it pure, no longer is it true,
when you set limits to those with knowledge and hinder the God in you.

See, the truth will make a way, yes, the truth will find a face;
rather it's beautiful or ugly is based on your embrace.

And once the limits of learning are known, the class will sit in silence,
fully aware of your small stature in comparison to a giant.

Surely, you're just mad because I thought of it first;
the truth is, I just bumped my head on the ceiling, and it hurts!

It's Hard to Be Humble and Cocky at The Same Time

I try to come off humble because I don't want to offend you,
but that's not real humility, for me to be the pretend-you...
See, when I let my light shine, I reveal to you your glory;
and should my truth be told, I'd reveal to you your story...

I have to say, it's hard being humble and cocky at the same time;
because we will find nothing agreeable without sharing the same mind!

I must admit, I'm here to serve you in hopes to make *us* better
but, it's hard for me to serve you if you think my mind 'lesser'...

I'm trying to tell you something, but you won't give me the time;
you won't afford me the opportunity, you reject me by design.

I'm trying to submit to you without giving you a piece of my mind,
but it's hard being humble and cocky at the same time!

My frustrations bubble over, and I forget to be patient;
realizing you're just not there yet as I fly off in my spaceship...

I guess, to deny my own intelligence is for me to be down to earth;
I guess, teaching you is irrelevant if I don't put *us* first...

So, even though you disrespect me and forget me to shine,
I know that we will find nothing agreeable without sharing the same mind.

Truly, it's hard to be humble and cocky at the same time...

In Time, All Things Will Be Perfected Because Your Timing is Perfect

There is a thorn placed in my flesh, and to remove it is urgent!
But on the contrary, you, oh Lord, say I deserve it.

Because, in time, all things will be perfected, your timing is perfect...

Your grace is sufficient, my willpower isn't;
so, I must adhere to your grace more than my wisdom.

Because when I am weak, then he is strong;
you're making me weak for whom I belong.

Yes, I plead, and I beg that you change your decision,
and remove this pain that pokes with precision!

This thorn in the flesh is an ache to my heart,
a pain to the death, for which I depart.

It dampens my fire, it is dimming of hope;
yet you see it as good, the fruit of my soul!

Because I am great, great burdens I bear.
Though I'm alone with this pain, you're always there.

To show me my weakness is making me strong,
this thorn in the flesh is to spur me along...

Though I feel as if I do not deserve it,
you assure me that one day it all will be worth it...

Because, in time, all things will be perfected,
your timing is perfect...

Unto The Promise

Unto the promise does my hope belong;
in this promise, I am made strong.
All my strength, toward 'his will complete,'
I gird myself with a heavy-deep!
My sword is Truth my shield is Faith,
I go to war assured my fate!
His mercies are from everlasting;
his wondrous works, my heart surpassing!
I give unto him all my strength,
for he is worthy though I faint.
My heart takes great courage in light of the hope I see;
I run into battle courageous, sure my victory!
He is my protector as I cling to the innocence of his cause,
he is my perfecter amidst the lion's jaws!
I need not boast I need not brag,
his voice does keep me humble;
I run the race at any pace,
his word says I won't stumble…
Those with power, those with pride
do not see when hearts divide.
But the God I serve sees it all,
he saves my feet from their fall.
His word alone is my protection;
his voice is strong, his strength a lesson!
I fear him and only him,
by his command is my direction;
by his promise, my perfection!

CHAPTER 5

The Living Word

He Guards His Word with His Life

The tension in the air is thick enough to cut with a knife
but he will speak no wrong, for he guards his word with his life!

For the wickedness of their ways, he will pay the ultimate price,
yet he will say nothing of it, for his tongue speaks what is right.

As a sheep led to the sheer as a lamb led to the slaughter,
desolation is ever near, yet he sets his eyes to the father.

As blood drops from his beard, he sweats grief in the garden;
hands folded together; his word mustn't depart him.

Feverishly praying:
"Lord, may this bitter cup pass from me!
Nevertheless, you know what's right,
so thy will be done, oh Lord, even on this night!"

For the wickedness of their ways, he will pay the ultimate price,
yet he will say nothing of it, for his tongue speaks what is right.

The tension in the air is thick enough to cut with a knife
but he will speak no wrong, for he guards his word with his life!

The Promise is Real

I didn't see the holes in his hands but, the promise is real!
I know it in my heart that that is just how he feels,
to take a brutal beating and then carry that cross
up to the top of that hill, spilling blood as he walked…

See, he was on a mission, a man with a vision;
he knew that we were watching, so he was a witness.
To show us he understands all the pain that we feel,
he came down to earth and went through our ordeal;
so that we could trust his word and know the promise is real.

Now, I wasn't there when it happened but, I've been told of the story
of a man with holy hands who descended from glory!
They say that he walked on water,
they say that he raised the dead,
they say that he was killed for the simple things that he said.
He spoke the truth in love even to those who wouldn't feel;
he couldn't do any faking because the promise is real!

He had to be true despite the evil they'd do,
they thought he'd walked into a trap, but he already knew.
See, he gave them his life just so they could test him,
waited in the garden all night so that they could arrest him;
drag him into court for a chance to confess him…
He knew that he'd be mocked and that as a king, they would dress him,
crown his head with thorns and seek for him to impress them…
All along, he wasn't shocked by their misdirected zeal,
their hopeless determination, or their manipulative skill.

He came for this very reason: so that the truth could be revealed;
he brought hope down to earth so that the promise could be real!

Now, we know how the story goes, although I've never seen the holes,
they nailed Him to that cross, blood dripping from his toes!

They took him down, wrapped him up,
and though his tomb had been sealed,
an angel rolled the stone away,
he rose that third day,
and the promise was real!

When the Truth Comes Along

How will you react when the truth comes along?

Will you welcome it to your house? With you, will it find a home?

Will you curse it at the door; will you shut the door in its face?

Will you hear, with an open heart, what the truth has to say?

When the word became flesh, don't you know, we all saw the way;

the multitudes thronged him and pleaded with him to stay,

self-important men wronged him; prideful men shunned him away,

some, with indignation, looked upon him with hate:

one look at their reflection, and they couldn't stand to see his face.

But, how will you react when the truth comes along?

Will you recognize its power before the truth hits your home?

Will you kneel at its seat and, with your hair, wipe its feet,

or will you question if it's real and enquire of what it thinks?

Would you go along with the truth, would you obey its every command?

Would you step onto waves of water and take the truth by its hand?

Would you confess the truth is God if he asked you who he is?

If you betrayed the truth, would you warm yourself in shame?

Would you deny knowing the truth if he called you by your name?

If you betrayed the truth and sold the truth for a lie,

how would you live with your deception if you caused the truth to die?

If the truth did die and somehow came back to life,

would you believe the truth is living when they tell you he's alive?

If the truth met with you briefly to tell you that the world was free,

that he paid the price for sin, but he needs you to help them see,

how would you respond, now in the knowledge of right and wrong,

convinced that God is real and knowing the truth is strong?

When the word became flesh, we all saw the way,

yea, the truth and the light were made clear as day.

Although the truth died, that doesn't mean he's gone;

one day he's coming back; he's coming back to bring it home!

So, how will you react when the truth comes along?

Jesus Felt Alone

Of a truth, Jesus felt alone;
way before the cross, he was on his own,
thinking,
"Dang, I'm really in this by myself;
if I'm here to save the world, who can be my help?"

Probably felt like giving up, probably felt like crying;
way before the cross, he hung there dying...
In a world of pain where trust slowly fades away
truly, he was crucified day by day.
He had no friends, none on whom he could depend.
He was a loner from his birth unto the very end,
thinking,
"Dang, I wish I had someone who understands
that one day I will die for the sins of man."

They say it's lonely at the top: he was the king of kings;
no doubt he felt less than a human being...
While superior to his peers, he was all alone;
yea, way before the cross, he was on his own.
Of a truth, Jesus felt alone...

He Made It Understandable

He put it in a way that is hard to deny,
wrote the message on our heart so, our heart would reply...
He sent a gift so precious it'd make a grown man cry;
he made it understandable, giving his only son to die.

Because we had a hard time grasping it and seeing the bigger picture
he delivered us a message that would forever deliver!

He came down to our level to reason with us
and he gave us all that he had in hopes of gaining our trust.

Some still question him today because his message isn't tangible
but when I say, "he gave his only son to die..."
Just know,
he made it understandable.

Pouring out his blood, his sweat, and his tears
he displayed his love for you so you could see it for what it is.

Now when the message of his love reaches you
I pray it breaches you!
I pray you are not brutish as an animal...
but seeing that he gave his only son to die,
he made it understandable...

CHAPTER 6

Living in Sin

Faint Hearts Cry

Faint hearts die amidst the rose pedal's bloom;
the long-lost cry in a peaceful lagoon.
As storm clouds brew, as the wind blows warm;
the rain won't drop until the last sung song.

Through the dry-parched desert does the foreigner strand;
in the sunbaked heat travel seas of sand.
As the lone wolf cry does the strong man die;
far from his home, cleaving to his 'why.'

Out the old wooden frame does the orphan see shame;
through the window of his soul is the world's worst pain.
To be alone in the world and to wonder as to why
is the world's worst feeling, as do faint hearts cry...

Ties

Yeah, we may have a deal:
although I'm locked in a contract, my fate still ain't sealed.
Who I am, has not been revealed:
you don't know me, and you don't own me;
you didn't make me; therefore, you cannot take me.
As the father of lies, of course, you can fake me,
but since my father is God, the truth will never forsake me!
See, my father, he loves me way more than you hate me,
and his power to save me is stronger than your power to break me!
Although you got me signed on like a slave,
in the end, to your will, I will not cave!
I know you want to keep me trapped in a grave,
but the grave can't hold me or the one who breaks every chain!
You've got me tied up in past mistakes, it's true,
but one day, I'll meet the one who makes all things new!
He'll throw away my past mistakes and do away with you too!
Although you deny it; where there is a will, there is a way.
I refuse to believe my ties to you can bind up his grace!
Yeah, there's hope for a soul like mine!
Just give it some time, and I'll see the sunshine like I was truly designed!
So, what...?
You say I got ties to your lies…
the same is still true for his promises too!
Yeah, we may have made a deal…
Although I'm locked in a contract, my fate ain't sealed.
Who I am, has not been revealed:
you don't know me, and you don't own me.
You didn't make me; therefore, you cannot take me.
As the father of lies, of course, you can fake me,
but since my father is God, the truth will never forsake me.

Happy

A joy that I can't explain...
Happy, must my heart remain.
Being strong, I strain to smile;
to suppress the sadness,
to push it down.
I'll just stuff these feelings into my gut,
they must not reach my face;
lest someone sees that I'm unhappy,
lest they know of my disgrace.
I must be perfect
so as to bring perfection to those I see.
Because if I am happy, then they are happy;
so, happy, I make-believe...

'Truth...'
What is 'Truth...?'
I make-believe a lie,
I disguise the truth because it's ugly;
therefore, its face, I hide.
The last time I made known the truth,
my face began to cry.
To show my hurt, for all it's worth,
is to confess that I have lied.

The Silent Suffer

My aches and my pains,
I restrain them daily;
I suppress my feelings,
I withhold my cravings.
My lips stay closed
my hurt I cover;
my pain is real,
but the silent suffer.

I beat myself,
I purge my heart;
my love, I hate
till hope depart!
Invisible tears
remain unseen;
there's no remorse
for silent screams...
My vision blurs,
my thoughts distort;
my dreams do die
with no support.
My cry is faint
though words, I mutter;
it's no surprise, the silent suffer.

A Fool's Promise

There is no promise for a fool
because although he knows what's right,
he is void of understanding, and his way is void of light.
He walks a dark path, knowing not which way he goes.
His journey seems prolonged as he stumbles the dark roads.
The darkness of his way holds no reassurance;
he has left the paths of life with no chance of endurance.
He continues in his sins, knowing his way leads to death.
He drinks his bitter cup, growing more wicked each step...
Yes, the promise of a fool is no promise at all;
blind and without knowledge of his way, he shall fall.
Lest he returns the way he came, he shall wander and roam;
lest he backtrack and repent, he'll never find his way home.

Turn back, oh fool, follow the trail of your bones;
see all the life you have wasted, see all the things you've done wrong.
Stop your feasting, oh fool, turn from your destruction;
gather the things that you've lost on this path of corruption...
In your gathering of this evil, you'll see the truth you must face;
in your disgust for what you've done, may you recover your grace.
In the distance shines a light that grows bright with each step;
repentance is the way you so foolishly left.
As you draw closer to this light, you will uncover your fears,
and with each step that you take, your path will slowly appear.
As the light grows brighter, may your vision return;
and as your spirit rises higher, may you live as you learn.
Soon you'll understand, as your heart becomes honest,
the beauty of a path for a fool with no promise...

Transgression

It is a nasty and dirty feeling when you know that you've done wrong.
You can't explain yourself, there is really no excuse,
and now there's nothing left to do but face the cold truth!
You feel afraid because you know God saw everything you did;
you feel distant and empty like a fatherless kid.
The fact is you have a father, but you fear the day he shows up
because he promised to raise you right, and he will show you that love's tough.

He chastens his children; he disciplines those he loves.
So, now you're waiting on this whooping, nervous than a mug.
Knowing you got it coming because of the test that you failed,
you can only cling to your confession, realizing you broke the law;
fully aware of your transgression, knowing he sees all...

Only God Can Judge Me

When it's all said and done, only God can judge me;
your opinion of 'myself' cannot 'down' or 'up' me.
Who says the truth hurts and that it's always ugly...?
Sometimes, the truth feels good; sometimes, it hugs me!
You may doubt me and my current position,
but it's a good thing your feelings don't control his final decision.
Yeah, you can say what you want to say and feel how you want to feel,
but it just isn't in your power to heal or to kill.
Despite all your efforts to sway me,
you don't have a heaven or hell to place me.
Only God can judge me; only the truth can shape me;
not his truth or her truth but the truth that raised me.
Yeah, you might be frowning on me now because I'm in this season,
and you may think there's no way out judging by your reason.
But even while you doubt, someone's believing.
See, there's someone who forgives all the while that you sin,
and there is someone who is faithful all the while you condemn.

One who has unreliable friends comes to an end,
but there's a friend that loves you and sticks closer to you than a brother;

I'm so glad that only God can judge me...
because to you, I'm just an ugly duckling,
but to him, I'm a beautiful swan.
Although I look bad now,
he knows I'll change in time.
No, your words can't stain
what he has made to shine:
only God can judge me!

Why Do I doubt

Why do I doubt; why do I question what you're about?
As if the glory of your presence has not made the dumb to shout?
As long as you are inside of me, for what reason is disbelief?
Your thoughts are as my thoughts, so you inspire me to think.
As soon as the words have left my mouth, I am amazed at what you bring.
There is none more clever; you make my heart to sing.
You are the highest of the high, and to the lowly, your spirit clings.
Who brings laughter from the mouth but the same that makes to mourn…?
Why then do I doubt when, for you, my spirits torn?
You are the master of the clay, the shifter of the shape;
you make the lowest lows, and the heights do you create!
By you, an oasis is prepared and a desert place;
as long as I am yours, Lord, hold me with your grace.
Teach me endless love: how to withstand all hate.
You are the potter of this vessel by you I bend or break.
I remember, Lord, you told me not to question your glory;
all I have to do is trust you, but if I doubt, that's a different story…
No wonder it's impossible to please you without faith;
because in my search for great, it turns out that faith is all it takes!
Because I do not test you, you are testing me instead.
So that I may learn through trial and tribulation how one might get ahead!

Maybe one day I'll learn to put good to use;
to seek you where all I go, to hold you in all I do.
Although my fears were great, each time, you've proven true!
You've brought me all this way so, how far can I go with you?
Doubts are only 'worries'; my only worry is an excuse;
so why then do I doubt?

It Feels Good to Cry

It feels good to cry,
it feels good to let it go;
after holding it in for so long,
it feels good to let it flow.
It's like the breaking of a damn,
it's like the waters of a flood;
when tears come running down,
it's like a blessing from above
Yes, I cry,
and I cry,
and I cry,
and I cry...
until my tears finally run dry,
until my heart finally knows why,
until my soul has peace inside.
It feels so good to cry:
to finally let the old man die,
to finally let my spirit rest,
to finally free what was depressed,
to finally be what I've suppressed,
to finally see what had me stressed.
It feels so good to cry...

These golden tears, they mean so much;
held in for years, now they erupt.
As volcanoes spewing ashes,
as the wind stirs up the dust,
as a cloud heavy with rain,

as the sun from dawn to dusk;
it feels so good,
its freedom do I trust:
it feels so good to cry!

Angry Fool

The decisions of an angry fool are clouded beyond reason;
possessed with such hatred, he feeds his own demons.
He forsakes his prayer and seeks his own device
to change the course of things, although he isn't right.
Pain becomes his passion, his pleasure a twisted game;
he walks without a vision; he shoots without an aim.
His anger is a fire consuming his very life;
blinded by his fury, his destruction shines bright!
His light grows dim in the darkness of the night.
What sorrow awaits this man drowning in his pool;
tears can only wash him clean, for he is an angry fool.

Payback

God, I've been a hypocrite; this is a fact.
You forgive me of my sins though I put on an act!
I don't love em' as you love me, it's really a shame
how I front like I'm good when I'm really to blame...
Your forgiveness really should bring me to change,
but when it's time to forgive, I leave em' to hang.
To be a better person should be the impact,
so, instead of being worthless, I'm paying you back!

Those who treat me like crap, I'll start treating them better;
those who dare to tear me down, I'll be putting together.

I'll be praying for my enemies, loving all them that hate me;
showing them forgiveness, knowing you forgave me...

Cause I don't want to waste grace, seeing that you gave that!
Vengeance is the lords, so who am I to pay back...?

Submission

I can no longer anticipate hope,
expecting a measure of 'cope.'
In the background of sorrow, I grope;
to the songs of sadness, I wrote:
I submit...
Let it be known in the records, I quit.
For the hope of which I admit
was never my mission to get;
I submit...
I give in to the wind and rain
as a boat up against hurricanes,
thrust to and fro by the waves,
feeble to seasons of change:
I submit.
Forgive me but never forget.
I have come to the end of my wit
as an iceberg comes to its tip,
as an old man walks with a limp;
may the last words fall from my lips
be of one whose shoulder is chipped.
I submit.
I can't win; against whom have I sin,
when I finally give way to the end...?
I submit.

Satan Disguised as God

After finding knowledge of the way,
which master shall I obey?
Though I know the truth to be right;
in my knowledge, I hid from the light.
I hid because of my sin,
concealing the truth deep within.
Now, as the dark is dimming of light,
my mind is misleading of men.
The fear of man is a snare;
Uncover the truth if you dare,
but let the enlightened beware
that God has called us to share.
The rebellious deceive with their trust
learning how best to disgust,
covering their hearts full of lust
with knowledge of God so robust.
A people who have long since forsaken the way
have mastered how not to obey.
Now void of true peace of mind,
they rob others of natural design.
Those looking for insight may shine,
but the knowledge of wrong is a crime.
Led by way of the blind,
God, has Satan disguised.

The True Exploiters of Grace

The true exploiters of Grace:
make their home in the deepest parts of the heart;
clothe themselves with compassion;
while ripping their souls apart.
They feed on the trust of the meek,
live on the lies of the weak;
as wolves devouring sheep,
low to the earth, they must creep...
The true exploiters of grace
refuse to cover their face.
They stand bold, as one to be proud.
While wiping the blood from their smile,
they claim the life of a child.
Of the innocent, they have their fill;
the exploiting of grace is their skill,
to use the favor of God
as a cover for all of their lies.

Docile Brows

Those eyebrows stay raised high; they won't bend with concern.
You'd look me dead in the eyes and lie,
to swear that you're 'learned.'
But, with wisdom cometh sorrow,
so please, let's not pretend;
cause I can see it in your eyes,
that your eyebrows will not bend.

You will not stop to question nor change your disposition.
You hold firmly to your views;
eyebrows stuck in poised-position.
Your forehead is wrinkled from their raise,
and they do not rest to wonder.
For should your eyebrows bend
they'd have thought to ponder.
They stay risen in your strength:
eyes wide with pride,
but the humble still seek God;
as meek brows dive.

Their joy is true joy;
and when their eyebrows raise,
it's because they seek God
to the end of their days!
When your eyebrows don't bend,
your pride won't give way to your heart;
But one who is truly wise
will find that sorrow is smart.

Playing With Fire

At times, it's hard to let go of the destruction you're holding.
We often play in our sin till it leaves us smoking;
knowing good and well of our reason for pain,
staying the same in our season of change.

If the nerves of our soul were like the nerves of our body
we'd be better people; holy and godly.
For the spirit of God warns us from within
that we will be burned if we play with our sin.

"Be patient," he says, "let go of desire.
Danger is near; quit playing with fire!"
I know of your pain; I feel that your hurt;
but you're holding destruction; let go of it first.
Then shall I heal, then shall it please
to free you of sickness and cure your disease.
No, I cannot heal as long as you hurt;
by playing with fire, you're making it worse!
But if being burned cause' you to turn,
then you shall be healed as soon as you learn
to control your desire.
Danger is near;
quit playing with fire!

Behold, The Shattered Remains of a Broken Man

Behold, the shattered remains of a broken man...
Collecting the pieces of his past, he will do the best that he can
to shape the form of his future within the clay he creates;
to finally master the pieces of a life of mistakes...
Life hasn't been easy, so perfection is hard.
Mentally, he is damaged; emotionally, he is scarred.
He knows that to overcome, he must perceive a new perception;
should he be wise in his eyes, see the light in his own correction.
But to finally see the truth, he must seek out all of the pieces.
The lost parts of his soul are his deepest and darkest secrets.
Yes, he must seek a new direction; in a different light, his own correction.
Behold, the shattered remains of a broken man...

Lord, Make Me A Better Man

Lord, make me a better man,
Lord, fix me from where I stand.
My charming smile may have so many fooled,
but on the inside, it's cold and cruel…

Lord, make me a better man…
Truly, you see the heart of me,
and as I see the heart you see,
I am convicted and struck with grief
because I am not what I thought to be…

Lord, make me a better man;
if anyone can do it, I know you can.
Remove from me a selfish whore,
put in its place a faithful core.
Take away from me idolatry
so I can serve the God in me…

So long, I put myself as first;
no longer do I want this curse.

Lord, make me a better man…

I have much to learn, I must confess,
but, Lord, may life come from my death.
Crush my pride, direct my steps;
obey I will, with all that's left.
Lord, make me a better man.

False Believe

I'm mad I chose to believe what would deceive:
I'm mad at them, at him, and I'm mad at me.
I had my hopes high as I looked to the sky;
I counted on God, trusting he would provide,
but the end result was far from what I expected.
I anticipated great, but my hope was rejected;
rejected by family, rejected by friends,
and last but not least, rejected by him.
Dare I say it; am I wrong for coming clean?
I gave my all to God, and I didn't gain a thing.
Now I'm crying out to him, but in anger, I scream;
thinking, this must be a joke, wake me up from this dream.
I often feel that I'm his object of ridicule,
like he led me by his way so I could fall and be fooled.
I'm sorry, God, but this is just how I feel.
I used to come to you with questions,
but now, answers, you don't reveal.
It's like you left me out here high, and then dry;
no purpose, no reasons, no real answers to why.
Still, I know that I'm wrong in the way that I feel
and my own understanding is far from what's real.
You don't care about money, and you don't care about cars,
so, when I ask you to bless me, you made my way really hard.
I swear I try to see the light in the dark of this tunnel;
that while I seem to waste away, you are holding the funnel,
but optimism is tough when there's no easy way out,
and I have left off to believe; in belief, do I doubt.
Because when I tried, I failed, although, God, I held.

I feel like you let me go, but how can I tell?
I'm steady asking you for signs, like, "God, show me the way!"
But I might as well be blind because I always go astray…
You lead me to a dead-end; "Go on," you say:
you literally make me to trust you until my dying day.
But right now, I don't go because I have no faith;
I am useless to you, yet and still do I pray.
God, if I'm going wrong, please, tell me to stay,
and if I need to be moving, please, tell me which way.
I guess you kind of lost me when you said to jump to my death;
I stopped at the leap of faith, steady holding my breath.
To this day, I pray that your words don't deceive,
and that somehow, along this way, you can make me believe.

Inside I'm Crying

Inside I'm crying, though the tears don't come out.
Outside I'm lying, but the truth won't spew out.
I'm wondering how long I can keep this up,
I'm wondering if I'm at rest or am I truly stuck.
With no sleep, peace escapes me.
I'm working day and night for those who hate me.
I can't lie the thought of death sort of elates me!
Hope is hard to find with a spirit that breaks me.
Still wondering in my mind, why did God create me,
but it's different this time because I know he shapes me…
So, do I trust the potter's hand;
this man I am, will it stand?

Life's not bad, but I'm not jumping for joy;
I'm not eager for the day, so who am I faking for?
I know that at this rate, things will soon go downhill;
I made it to the top, but all for a cheap thrill.
I'm staring up at the stars looking for answers,
the stars are probably thinking, "he already has them…"
and inside I cry…

Oh, Wretched Man

Oh, wretched man, I see the sadness in your eyes;
the wickedness of your ways tells your tail full of lies.
You preach about freedom while you have yet to be free.
Look at the man in the mirror; tell me, what do YOU see?
Oh, wretched man, your pride and arrogance have led you astray;
in full knowledge of the truth, you still won't obey...
Count your cost and see if you can pay what you weigh;
you've *been* lost, so now tell me, what is your story today...?
Using the pity of others, you proclaim yourself strong; with cunning words
and crafty plans, you swiftly play them along.
God forbid, oh wretched man, that you admit that you're wrong;
but to die a lonely coward, there is nothing more wrong...
Your ways distort the truth; keep on telling those lies,
keep on selling those dreams; I see the pain in your eyes...
Throw on your shades in the day as you pretend to be bright;
portray a hero for morning and be a coward at night.
What strength do you really have, oh wretched man?
Allow the truth to unfold, and you'll see the blood on your hands;
that outside of sleep you have no rest
and that after life, there's only death
until this tale full of lies is all that's left.
You are misguided and misled
and you claim to know God's direction,
but you have yet to follow God
for you feed on your own deception.
Headstrong in your perception,
no one can tell you anything;
how will you ever learn your lesson?

I guess all that's left for you is a silent secret depression;
hidden from plain view, a truly sad obsession.
You worship only yourself, and you seek the praise of men;
it's no wonder you feel lost and separated from him.
The end of such a man, time will tell of his end;
the wickedness of your ways, oh most wretched of men.

Stumbling Block

There are things we put our trust in that are not God;
there are things that we run into before setting aside.
Now, the things that we depend on must have real strength,
and the things which we lean on must carry our weight.
So, in what we put our trust, we mustn't mistake,
and our God must be real; it cannot be fake!
Lest we try hard and fall to our shock,
lest we run into a stumbling block…

See, not everything is trustworthy,
not everything is for sure,
but we must examine the thing we trust
to know that it's pure…

For it to have real strength, it must have strength of itself,
but if it feed on our strength, it can't be much help.

There are things we put our trust in that are not God,
there are things, not trustworthy, that have a trustworthy disguise.

They are powerfully attractive; we fall in love with their charm,
but God says, "Only trust me, I will do you no harm."

Don't fall for the illusion of being on top,
lest the thing on which you stand be a stumbling block!

A real crisis reveals where you really put your trust;
now, is your hope found on high, or is it found in the dust,

because God is always ready to rebuild and restore,
but if your hope is not in God, you can never be sure.

If You're Not Being Tested

Go ahead, stack your money high to the sky,
but if you're not being tested, you should be wondering why...
You've got it "made in the shade" until the day that you die,
but if you're not being tested, you should be wondering why...

I saw a ruthless and wicked man flourishing in his land,
living carefree, yet he didn't understand
that for some life is hard for some it's as easy as pie,
but if you're not being tested, you should be wondering why...

Rather rich or poor, one should be tested on Earth.
Because Earth is the middle-ground and we are birthed from the dirt,
we should hope to be tested to uncover our worth!

Prisoner of The Mind

Held captive in a maze of my own design;
aimlessly wandering in the dark of my eyes blind.
I can't quite call it freedom by the way in which freedom is defined,
but this is a jail of my own making,
as a prisoner of the mind.

In the jail cell of my imagination,
such creations are abominations;
they are the undoing of my own life,
the mockery of my frustrations.

My futile attempts at freedom,
self-sabotaged by hatred
as the prison guards of regret and fear,
unto my hopes, have hasted.

They chained down my truth,
and when love was free, they chased it.
They bound my heart in locks of lies
to the ends that I embraced it!

Fortifying myself inside a fortress of solitude and safety,
I thought, "hope can't find its way in here; never again shall it break me!"

Deceived by my own design,
I starved myself of the food I need;
depriving myself of water
and of 'any reasons to believe.'

I made enemies of my friends
for the sake of nursing fear.
It seems that one has lost his mind
when 'sickness' he now holds dear.

Sadistic and calculating was a cruelty of my design,
yet no bars and chains appear to a prisoner of the mind…

The Test of a Man

What is a man made of;
what makes up a man?

So much pain does he feel;
so much his heart cannot take!

Days, he spends in anguish;
nights, without break!

He looks toward his mission
and confirms his decision;
to follow through with such pain,
he grants the permission
to let life ruthlessly shape him,
bend him and break him…

So many days he wants to die,
so many nights he wants to cry!

If only he could fly far away from his decay;
if only he could die and awake to another day.

Will he fail or prevail, is the question at hand,
yet only he knows the answer to the test of a man…

Talking Up a Storm

You just won't shut up, will you? Your mouth just keeps going;
speaking all kinds of things into your life without knowing…
See, if you truly knew, then your words would be few.
If you had confidence or knowledge that what you're saying is true,
well, then you wouldn't feel compelled to bump your gums as you do.

I want you to know that your words are destroying your soul
and until you keep your word, you'll be killing me slow…
See, 'real' recognizes real, and I understand the way that you feel,
but if you think that by talking up a storm, your words will seal the deal….
I'm sorry, but you're sadly mistaken;
there's an error in your system, and your circuit is breaking.
Your words are the wind, the thunder, and rain.
look at the mess that you're making; you're creating your pain:
talking up a storm!

CHAPTER 7

Testify

Suicide Prevention

When I was young and didn't know 'me' you tried to get me to kill 'me';
before 'the truth,' I was beholding, before discovering the real me.
Now, your goal is that this poem never reaches a young person's ears
because for one of them to discover themselves is the sum of every one of
your fears!

My journey to self-discovery was one of epic proportions;
I nearly saw the end of my life in search of what was important!
Your prayer both day and night was that, of your lies, I would never break
free.
So, you attacked when I was insecure and unsure of the real me!
Oh, you had me disguised, you held me in lies that in me was never the key,
so, I doubted myself, my heart I despised, and my truth I never believed…

If you'd have had it your way, my very life, you'd have prevented!
You were determined to lead me astray from the truth;
you were determined to leave me unfinished!

Yeah, when I was young and didn't know 'me' you tried to get me to
kill 'me';
before 'the truth,' I was beholding, before discovering the real me.

No, I didn't know how great I was;
of course, to you, it didn't make a difference…
because to you, I will always be a hopeless cause,
but now hope is the *cause* for which **I'm living!**

You Can Take My Life, but You Can't Take My Purpose.

You can take my life, but you can't take my purpose!
I will be what I was meant to be!
That's why I lay down my life,
so you can see what you were meant to see…

Now, I'm here for a reason; now, my reason is for a cause;
and should it take me my entire life, I won't stop for a pause!

Can't you see that I'm ready to do this for life!
I'm committed to it for eternity; that's why I give it my life!
So, whatever comes first, hell or high water,
it doesn't matter, it won't work, it won't deter, so why bother?

Because I finally found what I am meant to do,
up until the day I **die**, I will see it through!
There's something that I'm living for that dwells beyond the surface;
it takes real heart to pursue it; it might get ugly before it's perfect…
Either way that it goes, I won't be shaken; I'm not nervous.
Because you can take my life, but you can't take **my purpose!**

Fear not who can harm the body but who can harm the body and the soul in hell!
Your hate is just fuel to my fire; you make a pure purpose prevail!
You think that by taking my life you took my purpose; well, that's swell!
Because after life, we'll all see the *true purpose* that **only time can tell!**

You Made Me Live

Right where I should've died, Lord,
you made me live;
Because of you, I am alive, Lord
for thanks to give!

When I was strung out on weed, Lord,
you held me back
from going down a harder path
and smoking crack!

No doubt there have been moments
when I thought that I was through,
but those moments are now memories
and it's all thanks to you...

Because where I should have gotten worse, Lord,
you made me better;
when I thought that I was cursed, Lord,
you were a 'blesser.'

Night and day I cried, Lord,
no care to give;
yet right where I should've died, Lord,
you made me live.

When I was depressed, in the anguish of my soul,
I thought to take my life,
I thought that you would never make me whole,
but in the depths of all my sorrow,

you reached in and pulled me out!
Now I see tomorrow, and I know without a doubt…

that it's because of you I am alive, Lord,
for thanks to give…
Because right where I should've died, Lord,
you made me live.

Lord, when times were hard: a wall against my back,
bills above my head: at work, I'd eat a snack.
My heart would melt within me.
I thought it'd always be this way;
struggling to survive living day by day.
But Lord, you see my future in the midst of where I'm at
You gave me *provision*; how can I ever pay you back…

Because right where I should've died, Lord,
you made me live
It's because of you I am alive, Lord,
for thanks to give.

No doubt there have been moments
in my life when I was stuck,
but these moments are now memories
because you pulled me from the muck.

You made me live in these moments
where, no doubt, I could have died,
so that I could live each moment
knowing that you're alive.

Yes, right where I should've died, Lord,
you made me live;
it's because of you I am alive, Lord
with thanks to give!

Temptation

I know what's right, but still, it's a fight.
Just to keep from doing wrong, it takes all my might.
How can it be so simple and yet so hard?
God, promise me that if I trust you, my heart, you'll Guard.
The enemy is so cunning he wants to steal me away,
but God, don't let it be, don't lead me astray.
I need you now more than ever; my spirit is 'broke,'
I feel so hopeless inside; Lord, restore my hope.
What goes around comes around that is the circle of life;
please, stop me from doing evil that I may receive what's right.
Because to keep from doing wrong, it takes all my might,
and although I know to trust you, still it's a fight...
Give me strength for this temptation; Lord save my life!

Tears Of Joy

God, I can't ever remember being so happy and grateful that I began to cry.
Tears of fallen down my face before, but always for a different reason why…

but for the first time in forever, I saw joy through the pain,
and sure enough, tears came pouring down like clouds heavy with rain!

At the time, I thought something was wrong with me
I didn't realize something was right…
that you've been on this journey all along with me
that you've kept me all my life…

God, you are more than a friend to me;
for me, your love runs deep…
So much so, that my eyes begin to water
as tears flow down my cheek…

I could've been dead,
I could've long ago lost my life.
I could've quit; I could've given up;
I could've lost my will to fight…

Last night felt like surgery on my soul;
I never knew tears could feel so good,
I never knew crying could make you whole…

…I never knew how much you understood…

See, for the first time in forever, I saw the innocence of this boy
who you have sheltered and protect,

who all the weapons in hell could not destroy!
And yeah, I cried... for the first time in forever, with no shame at all, I balled;
stopped everything I was doing like a car engine completely stalled...

I never felt so loved by anyone in this world;
never felt so precious, so valuable; never held diamonds or pearls...

In awe of your goodness,
all I could say was thank you!
While my wiping the tears from my face,
all I could be was thankful...

You Are with Me

The main objective of the enemy
is to put distance between me and you...
So, when I'm struggling with sin, of course,
you, he doesn't want *me* to run back to...
Instead, he wants me to hide from you in shame
like Adam and Eve did in the garden;
he wants me to cover up my sin
and pretend as if no one saw it.
He doesn't want me coming back to you for help,
he doesn't want my innocence reclaimed;
for me to be vulnerable and honest with you again,
naked and unashamed...
He knows the connection we have is like pure joy to my heart,
so to keep me bitter and angry, he tries to sever from the start!
Whispering 'every lie in the book,' he swears up and down that you don't
get me.
He fears the day that I realize you never left, but you are with me!

Devil, go back to the depths of hell where you came from,
you're just jealous of what God and I have,
because you know that as long as he is with me,
at all your lies, God and I laugh!

I know now that the last thing you want me to do
when I am truly going through
is open back up to God;
for me to, once again, be naked and vulnerable...

See, as long as I think God is judging me,
I'll be in the dark, not knowing who hit me.
And as long as I believe God is 'punishing,'
you'll swear up-and-down that God is against me!

God, I refuse to believe the devil's lies;
no longer will I question who sent me;
but the promise is true that whatever I do;
I finally see you are with me...

God Is Always with Me

God is always with me; I've come to this conclusion.
The devil won't deceive me, for his lie is an allusion!
At times, I sin, and suddenly, God seems so far away,
but God's love trumps our sin if only we should pray!
Acknowledging his presence in the midst of the storm
is like a silver lining amidst the clouds, a sun's ray to keep us warm.
I've come to the conclusion that God is always with me;
unto the ends of the universe, he will not forget me!
The real sin is to believe otherwise; yes, sin can leave us empty.
Of a truth, God is in us and, of him, there is plenty!
This feeling of abandonment, as if God has left,
is an allusion to the ends of which God will not accept!
Yes, sin does separate us from God, but God separates us from sin!
Now, no hand is strong enough to pry us from the love of God within!
No, the devil won't deceive me, for his lie is an illusion!
God is always with me; I've come to this conclusion!

God, You're My Only Friend

I have no friend but you;
when I'm not acknowledging you
I have no one to see me through…
It feels like everyone has gone from me
like I am completely by myself.
No one wants to talk to me
and no one wants to help.
It's like the people who I'd like to hear from
are the last to answer my call,
and I'm starting to feel
abandoned all in all.
I'm tired of being put off,
tired of being neglected,
tired of being disregarded,
and tired of being disrespected.
People are so quick to use me and accuse me
but no one wants to fill me up:
to hear my side or heal my pride,
to help me where I'm stuck.
It makes me feel like I have no one but God;
God, I have no one but you,
because you're my only friend,
the only one who will see me through.
When you fill me up
that's when those friends come back around;
the same friends that left,
the same friends that let me down…
But truly, God,
You're my only friend…

I Got Here by His Grace

Honestly, I have to say
his grace got me here;
just to breathe this air today,
by grace, my name was cleared.

I have no right to life
seeing, how badly I deserve death;
it's to my own surprise
that I still have a 'life' left…

I could go on all-day
about the evil of all my crimes;
should time permit me to tell you,
I'd tell you of whom permits me time.

He gives it to me in spite of me;
I am his object of disbelief.
People look at me saying,
"How can this be?
Surely, his life should cease."
To their surprise, I remain alive,
therefore, his name I speak!
My life's not mine; I cannot claim
what doesn't belong to me…

I have stolen so many dreams
and broken so many hearts,
it took me so many lives
to see my purpose sharp.

My life's not mine,
his grace is why
I live and why I'm free;
I am happy because he made me so,
for his reason, do I sing!
So,
when someone asks
what is my story
I honestly have to say,
that it's to his glory
that I'm still here...
I got here by his Grace!

CHAPTER 8

Church Hurt

Church Hurt

I'm tired of being strong; my love may turn to hate.
In this church, they treat me wrong while smiling in my face!

I've been taking beating after beating steady preaching this word,
but let me act a heathen; they'll look at me absurd!

They think I don't have feelings because I teach the word of God,
Still, I have to feel their feelings after mine have been deprived.

Emotionally, they crucify me, saw me in half, and boil me alive,
while from the verses of this book, I teach them how they may survive.
Ironically, I speak for their hope if, from God's word, I have spoke.
But as they desecrate my name, I fear that on my own words, I will choke!
These people need Jesus; they need God in the flesh,
the way they nail me to this cross and try to beat me to death.
How long shall I speak about love in the face of such hate;
unless I *be* about love, I will seal my own fate...
Cause' if you get pushed down enough times, you'll be ready to push back;
lash out in retaliation: from the pulpit, I might attack!
The same word used to build you up; I might use it to tear you down,
and if you don't read your word, you won't know the difference anyhow.
Instead of preaching about heaven, I might just condemn you to hell.
See, if my hope runs out, I wonder if *you can tell...*
Cause' I'm tired of being strong; my love may turn to hate.
In this church, they do me wrong while smiling in my face.

Oh, Thirsty Soul

If God moves you to pour into me, then may my cup be filled;
but as for me, shall I seek your container that my heart be healed:
God forbid, but unto God himself, I must bravely go
to kneel at the father's feet and drink for my thirsty soul…

Through many disappointments, I've learned that you and I are much the same.
Now, should we bear each other's soul, there'd be much to blame,
but there is one who bears our soul and carries away our shame;
he drank the bitter cup of death to wash away our stains…

I've come to the realization that truly we cannot be our own surety
and that 'two insecure people' doesn't mean security…
As I've grown older, time has shown me that we've all got room to grow;
but to be patient with one another is all the truth we know.
At times, we won't *have* to *give,* so unto God, we go;
he will fill our cup and wash our sin away, as white as snow.
He only asks of us a broken heart, for he is willing there to mend;
to heal us of a broken heart, he died for all our sins.

So, if God moves you to pour into me, then may my cup be filled;
but as for me, should I seek your container that my heart be healed:
God forbid, but unto God himself, I must bravely go
to kneel at the father's feet and drink *for my thirsty soul…*

Friends Fade Away

As true love disintegrates
common interests dissipate;
our hearts drift their separate ways
as friends slowly fade away.
When we were young love was easy,
and trust came easy too,
but now we're old, and we're cold
from all that love has put us through.
I look around me at who surrounds me
and I find that friends are few,
and although we're grown, our life has shown
that from love, we finally grew.
I do not reach out to them
to share the love that we once knew,
for the interests of our hearts,
we no longer will pursue.
I miss my friends, and I miss the times
when our hearts were true;
when we were young love was easy,
and trust came easy too.
But now, I just take it day by day,
no time for friends that fade away...

Where The Road Ends

Where the road ends, a new path begins;
we meet new people and make new friends.
All is well in life; in life, all is good.
Through the good times and bad, things go as they should.
Time tells all, and with all that time tells,
we see that time is a blessing and that existing is swell.
I can't complain about the 'now,' who knows what's later;
all I know is that I'm blessed and that things work in my favor.
Where one road may end, another path begins.
If we let go of our past and forgive all our sins,
we'll find that the road least traveled is the one with no end…

Some People, You Don't Want in Your Life

Some people you don't want in your life,
yet they are given to you anyway.
We have to deal with these people,
rather wrong or right;
it goes without saying,
some people you don't want in your life.
If they stayed away from you,
by far, to them, you'd be no use.
They blow you off consistently,
although you give them no excuse.
They have to be there
in order for you to grow;
they have to do you wrong
in order for 'right' to show.
Some people need security,
so, in their friends they find surety.
Beware, their intentions lack purity;
and some people you don't want in your life.

It's A Full-Time Job Keeping Hate Out of Your Heart

It's a full-time job keeping hate out of your heart;
it takes a whole lot of love because hate will tear us apart!
It's hard to understand; sometimes, we just don't get it.
It's hard to forgive; sometimes, we just won't admit it.
Ever been so broke that you don't want to get fixed;
ever been so pissed that you enjoy being ticked;
until you love the thought of hate like it's hate that makes you smile?
Take a second just to listen if you've been there for a while.
You wake up in the morning, and you can't get out of bed
without thinking of that person or the things that they said.
You go to work in spite, and with all of your might,
you try to stay focused from day until night.
It seems when a heart is heavy, a load is always ready;
moving that weight around makes it hard to hold steady.
It adds up, don't you know, rather fast or slow,
but you don't want to give in, so you refuse to let go.
You feel you took a worthy stand and that the time will come
that they will hang their head in shame and say, *"Job well done!"*
So, every day you wake, you throw it over your shoulder,
and every night you go to sleep under the weight of a boulder.
Now your summers are getting hotter, and your winters are colder;
your season is losing savor, and life has gotten shorter.
As much as you won't admit it, you can't wait till life is over,
so you can lay your burdens down and relieve those *cold shoulders.*
After all the work you've done and all the time that you've lost,
you realize you may as well have picked up *a cross!*

And if what you know now, you'd have known from the start,
you'd have given all the love you had to keep from tearing apart.
Because, though it's tough to forgive, and admitting is hard,
it's a full-time job keeping hate out of your heart...

The Truth Will Set You Free

I tried running from The Truth,
but The Truth found me;
I tried living out a lie,
but my life downed me.
You can't run from The Truth,
and The Truth won't leave;
the truth is until you love *it*,
you will never be freed.
To hate life is merely to hate The Truth;
"All who hate me love death,"
Proverbs 8:36.
You can kill yourself drinking,
and why should you die smoking,
rather than admit that
somewhere along the way, you stopped hoping.
There's a big difference between hoping and just coping.
The difference is happiness and peace from within.
Knowing that you were true reassures you a win;
knowing you gave your all to be a light to the dim;
knowing you upheld the truth, lifting your light to the sky,
escaping the darkest powers and evading a lie.
There is much truth to an old saying preserved in His-story;
there's no use in complaining of the terms of His glory;
no excuse for running from what your eyes clearly see.
Only a lie I can condemn you; chained up with no key,
but just trust there is a way, and The Truth will set you free…

Mercy Is a Choice

God shows mercy to whomever he pleases;
mercy is a choice; this is my thesis.
It's not based on merit,
nor determined by works,
but mercy is free,
grace is freely dispersed.
Often, we are offended
by what we do not deserve,
because mercy is lent
In a way that seems absurd.
We look to whom it's lent
and lose sight of the fact
that mercy is a choice
just as grace is an act.
God shows mercy to whomever he pleases
it's his choice to give grace,
and our choice to receive it.
He didn't have to *show us love*,
especially when we didn't deserve it;
it was his choice to be blind
in 'his making us perfect.'
Why do we question others blessings
as if we are cursed,
we should be happy that they received
what wasn't deserved.
If God went by the rule book,
if he did what was fair across the board;
if he didn't choose to show mercy,

we would all be destroyed…
God knew what he was doing
when he made the exception;
when he decided to show *mercy,*
and use *grace* as a lesson…
No, it's not based on merit,
nor determined by works,
but mercy is free,
and grace is freely dispersed.
Thank God, He shows mercy to whomever he pleases;
it's his choice to give grace,
and our choice to receive it…

Misleading Light

In a room full of lights, one light stands at the head;
his position, so prominent to the way he has led.
In the gathering of the lights, his shine is the brightest;
amidst the congregation of lights, his place is the highest.
But as fire has need of fuel, as lights need shine bright;
what is the source of his power, what is the cause for his hype?
Though he is the smartest one in the room,
though he seem great in our sight;
in a world full of darkness,
is he a misleading light?
Should all the lights of the congregation
no longer zealously court him,
would it lead to his demise;
would it soon dim and distort him?
For if he be bright, let him be bright,
not merely bright among others;
should there be source to his light,
should there be love between lovers...
God forbid, his light shine
when only *we* come together.
Heaven knows that such light
will not last forever...
We see him as the leadership of the people;
by his vision, our future is bright!
But if he be not bright for our future,
he is a **misleading** light.
Should we forsake the congregation
and go into the night;

will we find that he was wrong,
will we learn that we were right?
For he warned us of the darkness,
we were warned of the night,
that outside of this room
we would never find life.
Though he is the smartest one in the room,
though he seem great in our sight;
in a world full of darkness,
is he a misleading light?
See, in a room full of lights, one light stands at the head;
his position, so prominent to the way he has led.

Let Us Break Bread Together on Our Knees

Oh Lord, let us break bread together on our knees,
let us bear this cross together, let us, please!
You are my brother in the faith, and we may not always agree,
but I pray the Lord keep you, as he is gently holding me.
I pray that such contention might not last for us forever,
but I thank God most of all for holding us all together.

I stormed out on you the day that we departed from one another;
many years have gone by, and now I dearly miss my brother.

Through the good times and bad, your life has made me better.
Deep down in our hearts, we know that love can bear the weather,
so, we keep holding on to love just as God holds us together.

Now, I pray your spirit be at peace; I pray you know of my repentance.
Should we have ought against each other, the judge would give us both a
sentence.

For we both know the savior and the cause for which he bleeds.
So, let us break bread together, Oh Lord, *on our knees...*

Throwing Stones

You strike me down with bitter words;
your aim to kill me is absurd!
In light of my sin, that is known,
you hold nothing back in throwing stones...
You aim with such precision confident you will not miss:
you hit the *heart*, yet missed the *mark*;
perhaps you weren't *sinless*.
At this moment, you forget forgiveness,
so convinced you know the truth.
To strike one down, to take a soul,
seems Gods Goodwill to you.
As you pick up rocks of heavy load,
wound them up, and begin to throw,
you do it all in demonstration
of a truth you do not know.
With a vainglorious disguise, you hide the heart within;
to your demise do you devise evil plots with wicked men.
You feel that to secure salvation is to mark the one with sin.
And behold, as you point your finger
there are three that point within...
If there can be life in words, no doubt, there can be death,
and if the merciful man does well to his soul,
the cruel man troubles his flesh.

As the Pharisees drew their rocks,
Jesus drew a line upon the sand
exclaiming that he who is without sin
be first to curse the damned.

One by one, they drop their rocks,
for, surely, they all had known
that among them all, there was none
worthy of throwing stones.

Forgive Them

If your brother offends you, forgive them;
let go of the wrong that is *in them*.
No one is better than another, but we are all the same;
we all fall short of his glorious name.
Who is good but God; are we not *all* bad?
Who has never sinned, who has never been sad?
Are we not all sons of a forgiving dad?
Did he not give his son, did he not give his last?
Give forth what is true, offer up something right;
draw near to his presence, stand bold in the light!
The wrong we did yesterday we did while still living;
who are we to say our God has stopped giving...?
His steadfast love doth endure forever.
He is with us at our worst, believing that we'll do better.
Who is a righteous man, who truly follows the Lord:
he whose way is with promise, he whose way needs no sword...
If your brother offends you, forgive them;
let go of the wrong that is *in them*.
Blessed are the merciful, for they shall be shown mercy;
blessed are the meek, for they should be deemed worthy:
forgive them.

Level The Playing Field

Let's make this a fair fight,
let's even the odds;
let's level the playing field,
and show favor to both sides…
Because it rains on the just
as well as the unjust,
and his sun shines on both
the saint and the sinner,
let's be clear on one thing here:

everyone's a winner!

When Christ shed his blood on the cross,
dying for mankind,
do you really think he had conditions
to who his love might find?

Ask yourself,
what advantage do you have
if your love's not blind?
What conditions do you keep
where the sun don't shine?

Let's be fair about this thing:
we all fall short!
That means we all lose,
but don't be a poor sport,
because although we all lose,
through one man, we all win;

he came down to our level
to set us equal with him!

He shared his glory with us
to separate us from sin,
realizing that we were poor
and deeply troubled within…

He made it a fair fight,
he gave us a good deal;
he showed us a fair shake,
he leveled the playing field!

You see, he made us all special;
no, no one of us is the same.
So, when it comes to his grace,
just know that it's *not a game:*

You are no better than the next man
despite how good you feel,
for Christ set us all equal
when he **leveled the playing field!**

Get On My Level

Get on my level!
Don't make yourself higher or lower.
Get on my level!
Uplift yourself, but take that chip off of your shoulder.
Get on my level!
Let's see things eye to eye;
we all have one life to live, but one day, we all gotta die.
So, get on my level!
Help me to see it clear;
let's come together
so we can figure out why we're here.
Get on my level!
There's no time for playing tough;
let's get serious:
no one's better; no one's not enough.
Get on my level!
Let's be equal;
come on, let's be fair;
if you're in bad condition
my life is in despair.
Get on my level,
cause' we all need a helping hand;
no one's perfect, so we all ought to understand.
Get on my Level!

CHAPTER 9

Closer than a Brother

The Fairest Thing to Do is to Be Unfair

Try to see it from my point of view if you dare.
At this point, the fairest thing to do is to be unfair…

So long, we suffered without a soul to care,
but when no one loves you,
no one knows the load you bear.

There are those under the law and those above it;
to each his own, I say, to each his justice!

No, this poem isn't for those who pretend to care
but for those who seek what's truly good:

the fairest thing to do is to be unfair…

Yes, be exceptional: it's said that love makes us courageous;
I guess hate creates us cowards: both are equally contagious…

You can tell me I'm wrong all day,
but if I have never known or seen what's right,
then you are just another shade of grey
posing to be the light…

See, if no one's ever loved you,
then no one knows the load you bear,
and only God can judge
rather or not, you've had your share.

So yeah… on the surface, an eye for an eye just **seems** right,
but it's been said that he who has seen the heart of 'it' has also **seen** the light.

So long we suffered without a soul to care,
try to see it from my point of view if you dare.
At this point, the fairest thing to do is to be unfair…

It finally makes sense now why Treyvon just got life;
for a double homicide, they say that he died twice…

While at the same time Johnny just took his own life,
but no one seems to know the reason:
I guess he just didn't **like life**…

I guess that's why Christ gave up his life the way that he did,
to save everyone, from the self-righteous to the suicidal kid…

No, this poem isn't for those who pretend to care,
but for those who seek what's **really** good,
who want to know what's **truly** fair…

Try to see it from my point of view if you dare.
At this point, the fairest thing to do is to be unfair…

The Greatest Power Is Love

As much as I want to change you, you stay the same.
As much as I want to move you, you will not budge.
I am convinced now; the greatest power is love.
In hate, I saw your state wondering how I could hurt you,
but now I see it clear, that in love there is virtue…
I was so wrong in how I treated you, thinking it'd make you right.
It hurt when I defeated you, no clue who won the fight.
I have been swinging at the air and trying to choke the wind,
thinking you were the enemy when the enemy was within.
But now I see it clearly that the only way to kill you
is to be patient with you, nurture you, love you, and rebuild you.
Because tearing you down never worked,
and disgracing you made me ungrateful;
Oh, just think where you'd be now had I been faithful instead of hateful.
Yes, I finally found the key to truly making you cower!
At last, I am convinced
love is the greatest power!

The People You Love

When it comes to the people you love,
priorities change; you'll move things that won't budge,
mountains crumble in fear you'll go beyond and above.
Because nothing's too big for the people you love!

Doors will open, smoke will clear
for the ones you are you're holding dear.

There's a light through the dark if there's a son for the drear.

Love is strong, though it's blind; love is pure, love is kind;
if there are people you love, there's a hope you will find…

Though you carry a heavy load and you're stretched for your time,
in the power of love, your strength is defined!
Your patients may wear thin but keep searching within;
you'll find that all that you have is worth saving a friend…
Hatred brings the struggle, the fear, and the strife,
but with love, you breathe easy; in love, you'll find life!
There's a reason why at times, it's so hard to say no;
when it comes to those you love, your heart will always say go.
Mountains crumble in fear; you'll go beyond and above.
You'll do extraordinary things for the hope of a hug.
Nothing will be the same, none common or dud,
but everything will change for the people you love…

CHAPTER 10

Recollection of Revelation

What Is Hidden in The Light of God?

What is hidden in the light of God?
The glory of his presence goes beyond our eyes!
Have you ever tried your best to see into the sun;
one should go blind before the work is done!
Even the most awake folk are truly asleep;
even the most shallow folk are truly deep!
His glory goes beyond our eyes;
that's what is hidden in the light of God…
His brilliance, we catch a glimpse of it
as we strain to see the end of it…
But that we all should trust and obey;
in his presence, there are no words left to say…
Though we mourn and grope, "dark is the night,"
we know not what's hidden in God's light.

Our Spirit is Covered in Dirt

The flesh is deceptive by nature, but the spirit is truthful;
we so naturally cover with lies the one thing that's useful.
As toward his goodwill, we work,
we ponder the pain and the hurt;
as to why in weakness we cry,
as to why tears drop from the sky.
For we know the truth should come first
but our spirit is covered in dirt…

Oh, the dirt is deceptive indeed,
the grounds for corruption and greed;
from the pride of our shell, do we lead
while hiding the hope of our seed.
Now, as toward his goodwill, we work,
may we ponder the pain and the hurt;
as to why in weakness we cry,
as to why tears drop from the sky.
For we know the truth should come first
but our spirit is covered in dirt.
May the seed of common grounds grow,
laying our loftiness low.
Though the pride of our flesh be a show,
it seems only in death we shall know,
for our spirit is covered in dirt!

As We Get Older, We Make Mistakes

It seems as we get older, we make mistakes,
we grow stronger; we grow wiser
as we come to know God's Grace.
Youth is fleeting, and vain is beauty
as we stare death in its face.
We live, and we learn, with every day,
as we grow older, we make mistakes.
Throughout this walk of life
if there be anything we take,
it's that as humans, we will error
till we grow grey upon our face.
Yet, with each lesson learned
we are humbled by our hope,
that we can't live this life alone
because there's so much we don't know.
It seems we sought our independence
from the start-up of our days,
but as the days went by
we saw the error of our ways:
no one's perfect, we discern;
we're only human, we realize…
we need mercy, and we need grace
as we live and as we die.

As we grow older, we grow wiser; we learn more 'how to survive;'
that by his mercy are we living
and that his grace keeps us alive!

Look far into the future,
you'd be surprised to know your fate:
we grow stronger, we grow wiser;
as we get older, we make mistakes...

Stars

These tiny specks of light, so far out of our reach,
are zillions of miles away yet there for us to see.
As I tilt my head back, gazing at the night sky
I am amazed at constellations that connect with my eyes.
It bewilders me to fathom a creation so high;
captivates my imagination when I see them pass by.
I see the little dipper and her opposing big sister;
defiant in their opposition yet aligned with such precision.
Some shine bright white, and some with tints of red.
Some are very distinguished, and some are barely there.
It's hard to see them in the city; it's like they're hid from our sight,
but in the wilderness of open country is where their fire ignites!
It seems the darker the night, the brighter they light.
I feel a peace come over me when I consider their plight.
Some stars are grouped together like sisters or brothers,
while others stand aloof with the distance of cousins.
I see that they are many to we who are few,
I see they mean much to those with little to do.
It amazes me to think that our sun is just one of them,
holding the universe together, giving light to what is dim.
The stars inspire purpose, and their lights support life,
encouraging us to dream; with hope, they shine bright.
It's funny how we all see the stars, but each has its own view...
Sometimes I feel the stars sit and gaze at us too...

You Are One of The Stars

What from a distance seems small,
what from a distance seems tiny,
may be great in its future;
may be great in its finding.
When you compare yourself to others,
you look down from where you see;
and in that moment, you are tiny;
just as tiny as can be.
But when you look up at yourself,
you suddenly feel free
as you gaze upon a star
that you could very well be.
Little do you know you are one of the stars,
little do you know the very heavens gaze back at your show
and in mystery and suspense, the very universe beholds,
because you are one of the stars…

Never Thought of It That Way

My dad is finally letting me make my own decisions,
so, my heavenly father must finally trust my wisdom.

…Never thought of it that way…

Every day we have a choice to make,
and it's always life or death…

…never thought of it that way…

Since we all reap what we sow,
does that make the earth a giant farm?

…never thought of it that way…

If we are in the circle of life,
squares, triangles, and rectangles must all be deadly creations…

…never thought of it that way…

Is our *solar* system designed to maintain our soul?

…never thought of it that way…

My Mind is Changing the World, but This World is Not Changing My Mind

My mind is changing the world, but this world is not changing my mind;
a shift in focus is all it needs to adhere to my *natural* design.
Don't question my thinking as if my thinking is something that you should question.
But know, of a certainty, my mind is working to alter the 'end' you are destined!
This world is oblivious to my position
yet subject to my discretion.
So no, my mind will not be *known* of you,
but you will *know* at the end of my lesson.

I am a seed sown into the earth
to give birth to a new creation.
Of a truth, I am estranged of men and those of *common* aspiration.
They do not know from where I come from, nor my destination;
but God forbid I be discouraged by them, and they break my concentration.

I am free to choose my end; my end, I choose at any time.
So yes, my mind is changing the world, but this world is not changing my mind.

My God is Indestructible

What I fashion myself after;
the thing creating me
is truly indestructible,
although it's hard to see.
My values found where hopes abound,
though lofty eyes won't see:
I pride myself on nothing,
and nothing prides itself on me.
I won't be fooled into praising things
that find themselves corruptible,
but, my hope, it lies beyond the eyes;
my God is indestructible!
My pride and joy, you can't destroy,
my faith, you cannot fray.
While other Gods may bend and break,
my God shall always stay.
It is no *'thing'* that can be stolen,
nor can any take it away;
my God cannot be broken, molten,
or carved into any shape!
My God is matchless in every way,
your God may be unlovable:
he fashions me after himself,
my God is indestructible.

Take the Top Off Your Faith

When the sky cracks open and the heavens elate,
with eyes wide open, we will gaze at our fate!
To finally know the glory of God, our reality shakes:
the truth no longer concealed,
his glory finally revealed;
our minds obliterate,
our souls will elevate!

This may happen all in a day,
so why wait?
Do it now, and take the top off your faith!

As grains of sand upon the seashore
vibrate at the earth's quake,
many mountains cower and crumble;
these great stones shall not relate.
Break asunder, oh mighty mountains,
be cast down from the highest place;
be exalted ye lowly valleys,
be lifted and liberate!
May excitement fill your bones
upon such an occasion.
As the stirring of deep waters,
prepare for evaporation!
As the dew form on a blade of grass
from the morning's precipitation,
may the sun rise on all your glory
in its final evaluation;
awake!

Remember, this may happen all in a day, so why wait?
Do it now, and take the top off your faith!

Many truths be unknown
in the dim of the darkest night,
but the sun lies deep within us as the stars ever bright.
Be not bashful nor ashamed of your shining of light,
but as sparks form a flame, may your spirit ignite!
To finally know the glory of God, our reality shakes;
with eyes wide open, we will gaze at our fate
when the sky cracks open, and the heavens elate!

But this may happen all in a day, so why wait?
Do it now, and take the top off your faith!

The Love That Comes from God

In this world, this love seems odd;
how strange is the path we trod...
We *know* what cannot be seen;
what we've seen, our life describes:
to dwell in Jesus, to live in the love
of someone we never knew
is to be held captive by our hearts,
as imagination makes us new.

We draw strength from his strength;
from his story, retain our glory.
We are passionate about his purpose;
to his purpose, we are *affording*.
No doubt we're different;
no, we are not the same.
Since we learned from whence he came,
we bear our cross and lift his name!
We share his story and feel his pain.
In the impossible, our souls abide;
how strange is the path we trod...
Though in this world, it seems odd,
we've seen the love that comes from God!
We are witnesses of everlasting proof
to a world whose mind remains aloof.
We dwell in hope; we live in truth.
Our chains, we break; our bonds are loosed!

Lost Soul

Poor lost soul void of a home,
you are a mere phantom;
a ghost, you shall roam.

From God to nowhere,
from nowhere to God,
or from God to God,
should you open your eyes.

What is a man living in a world where he exists unseen,
where he can see with his eyes but cannot be seen...?
What is a holy ghost amongst mere men,
but a vision passing by or a fleeting from within.
We cannot see God, but we feel his presence;
in our heart, we discern his essence;
put to the test mere flesh, as we learn life lessons.
To what *ends* we find God is the thing in question;
while some will find God, seeing that from God they have Gone,
others walk blind, forever unknown.

Poor lost soul void of a home,
you are a mere phantom; a ghost you shall roam.

From God to nowhere,
from nowhere to God,
or from God to God,
should you open your eyes.

Time

These kids are growing up fast
as time seems to escape me;
working this nine to five
to catch glimpses of smiles on their faces.
In this world, time is flying.
In this world, time isn't forever.
The more time it takes to survive,
the less time we're spending together.
Such a paradox forces me to conclude
that time is the enemy of love;
Or should I say that it's money,
because *time* comes from above…
Yes, this world has gone mad,
seeing that it is running out of time;
but those who trust in eternity
will love the end that they find.
Though it's hard at times to discern
the *reality of time* I'm facing,
I must remember that it is **love**
and **not money** that I'm faithfully chasing.
Yes, memories of this life
will soon fade away.
My time on earth is short,
like the dawn of another day.
As I am rushing off to work
leaving my loved ones behind,
may their soul rest in peace
Knowing the value of their time.

The Audacity to Ask, The Audacity to Expect

People who have the audacity to 'expect' make a favorable impression upon God!

Those who refuse to ask don't share the same faith as those who refuse to be denied.

The truth is, God loves a challenge; the Bible says David was a man after His own heart.

No, he didn't keep quiet in the sight of the giant, but he arose as a light in the dark.

So arise, oh light in the dark, bring light to the darkness you fear;

question everything expecting an answer until everything's ever so clear!

Role Play

Since we already know how the story ends
you could call this life 'role-play,'
as we act out each scene, on the stage of life, each day.
From when the sun rises and the curtains open
to when the sunsets and the curtain closes,
it's a sold-out show, and no one knows it,
but the stage is filled with cheers and roses!
What a beautiful show, what roles we play;
what drama, what suspense, we live each day.

Where the Universe Ends, Our Being Begins

Unto the ends of the universe, we look to see
the origin of our making; to what ends we *be*...
With God, we have fellowship; we are more than friends;
so, where the universe ends, our being begins!

We become alive when we realize the ends of the universe.
When we see his face, we see that, by death, we can't be cursed.

As he reflects back to us the beauty of what he sees,
in the glare of his eyes, we find the beauty of our being:
that we ourselves are unlimited just as the universe has no limits,
that we could search God's heart for eternity and never find its ending,
that the thing that brings us to life is the thing we cannot see,
that we look at the night sky right before we begin to dream!

We peer into the deep, gaze at the unknown;
for to come into our being, is our inspiration shown...

As we come to understand that we are not alone,
in the vastness of the universe, we finally find our home.

Yes, love brought us to life, and love will keep us living;
to the ends of such a love do we discover our beginning!

See, with God we have fellowship;
yes, we are more than friends...

So, where the universe ends, our being begins!

When The Creator Calls

When the creator calls, he speaks through the mystery of our imagination.
His voice, like a bright idea, is cause for illumination.
When the creator calls, the heart of us shall listen;
as he calls out to his creation, we shall all bend in submission.
When the creator calls, we shall hurry without delay,
lest we miss our calling and are forced to stay the same.
His imagination does make us new.
How amazing is the imagination of the one imagining you...

Everything Hangs by A Hair of Faith

Everything hangs by a hair of faith;
by faith, everything hangs by a hair…
One wrong move is all it takes
for everything to fall in despair.

One act of faith is all it takes
to bring hope to many in despair…
and everything hangs by a hair of faith;
by faith, everything hangs by a hair…

With faith, you can move mountains,
without faith, mountains will crumble;
everything weighs in the balance
and nothing is spared from the trouble.

We walk by faith day by day;
we walk in the dim of the night!
Life is such a delicate balance
as we live by the thread of our life…

It doesn't take much for everything to collapse,
it doesn't take much for a fall…
swear by nothing, I say,
should you swear by anything at all!

There's Always Space for More Ideas

Hop in a spaceship with me;
God knows the journey we chart!
Conversation with me: two astronauts in the dark!

Now, before we go on this ride, let's make one thing clear:
there's always space for more ideas...

We search the galaxy, but astronomy and the telescopes don't know
that as far as the eye can see *is as deep as the heart can go!*

In a solar system, a man looks for his soul;
in a galaxy, a man peers from a globe…

Just a speck of dust floating around a blazing ball of fire,
Hanging off of the limb of an eight-legged spider…

It turns out the *'plan-net'* is a **'planned trap,'**
and the love of this world will hold your mind back!

You've got to see the bigger picture; stand in awe, and fear!

Yes, as you gaze at the night sky, notice this here!

There is always space for more ideas!

Those Fearful Moments Can Be Humbling, and Those Humbling Moments Can Be Fearful

What joy there is to the gullible,
and ignorance is truly bliss;
filled up with such hope and love,
the *doubt* they give their benefits…

But oh, what sorrow awaits their soul,
their joy need not be cheerful,
for those fearful moments can be humbling,
and those humbling moments can be fearful.

Teach a wise man, and he will be yet wiser;
rebuke a scorner, and get a blot;
some things that we should listen to,
we wish that we heard them not…

There is a subtle voice whispering
with deep secrets of old,
the brilliance of your future,
should you fear the truth as told…

His voice is soft and faint
yet hits home with deadly precision.
In the excitement of all we say to see,
is there life in our decision?

Lest we quiet our soul of excitement,
lest we humble our heart to be fearful,
we will not see the sorrow awaiting our soul;
that our joy need not be cheerful...
There is a reason to all our way,
and there is a purpose to all our paths.
In stumbling, shall we run;
in mourning, shall we laugh.
Pleasure is very pleasing,
but who is deserving of pain...?
The joy we sought and the pain it brought
are lessons that must remain:
embedded into our memories,
a stain upon our brain.
Pride cometh before the fall,
but in humility is no shame...

Lest we forget to be humble in the midst of being cheerful,
those fearful moments can be humbling,
and those humbling moments can be fearful!

CHAPTER 11

The End

The Last but Not the Least, The Least but Not the Last

We represent the home stretch; yes, we are the last call:
a generation of people, last but not least of them all!
As the world nears to an end, men seek for a friend,
so the Lord has left his chosen ones, on which the gospel depends!
Our faith: the end of a story; going out in a blaze of glory!
With heavy hearts, we march forward as clouds heavy with pouring.
The conviction of our soul, his revelation of glory;
the passion of our flame, the end of our world's destroying!

We gather much faith! Together, we bring many men to see,
in one moment of truth, of climatic extremity,
the hope of our soul which lies beyond the eyes;
the glory unknown, to the end we are disguised!

As fear has a death grip on the world, we are free indeed;
doing what seems strange, what many cannot believe!
Impossible is just a word to us, the ends of which we shall not know;
for unto us, all things are possible as unto God we go!

A lamp unto our feet, a light unto our path;
we are anchors of the human race charged with such a task:
To be the favor of God in a world that is slowly dying,
to stand tall in the wind to the hearts of men dividing!
That any man hear our plight that any perceive our call,
is our prayer both day and night as to our knees we fall!

For the victory, we run as the final hope of the team;
for should a dream come true, we must come true a dream...

Like gold that is refined amidst the fires blast:
we are the last but not the least,
we are the least but not the last!

Make Ready a Path for Our God

The dogs howl with resilience the moon,
gazelles leap with joy in their womb,
and as clouds prepare the monsoon,
deserts stir sands from their dune's...

"Make ready a path for our God!"

The trees stand tall in the wind,
volcanoes bubble within,
and as twisters from heaven descend
the turn of the world must begin!

"Make ready a path for our God!"

Hyenas laugh in the distance,
crabs crawl with persistence,
polar bears trudge through their blizzards,
and whales bellow their wisdom...

"Make ready a path for our God!"

There is coming a tide with the moon,
a night besetting our doom,
a day of skies ever clear;
with trembling, walk as in fear;
In desperation, be stranded;
repent in ways ever frantic.
Behold the cry of the planet:
the way of this world is abandoned!

"Make ready a path for our God!"

He Is a Holy God

Shattered and broken, our hearts divide;
devastated, crushed, distressed, deprived,
but he is a holy God…
Chaos and confusion on every side;
distortion and delusion infect the eyes,
but he is a *holy* God…

He is accountable for his creation;
his eyes are open to our devastation;
this is the comfort of our desolation;
yes, he is a *holy* God!

Though bleakness and gloom parade the streets
we mustn't assume our sure defeat;
right where we stand, he assures our feet;
in this journey called life, we must not retreat…
for he is a *holy* God!

no weapon formed against us shall prosper;
the curses on our life surely deserve an Oscar!
The wicked will not prevail,
we set the stage for his glory;
only time will tell the fruition of such a story…
for he is a *holy* God…

Therefore, I commit my life to his hands;
each step by faith is the mastery of his plan!
He is perfection, so perfection I am!

He is worthy, so I know that I can!
Yes, he is a *holy* God…

I count my losses, and I store my tears in a bottle,
send my issues to the Lord, and then it's not a problem!
Any issues that I had I could never solve em';
born into a world of sin: that's how I got em',
but he is a *holy* God!

Shattered and broken our hearts divide;
tainted, tortured, even traumatized;
chaos and confusion on every side;
delusion and distortion infect the eyes,
but he is a *holy* God!

We Did Not Come from Animals

The scientists are wrong, just as wrong as the cannibals,
we are born of God; we did not come from animals!
To say that we come from animals
is to say that we are on their level.
So, just as Satan entered the snake, now, we are full of devils!
It is easier to justify sin when you lower the expert expectation,
but God knew what he was doing when he set Man over creation.
Truly, nothing that God has made was meant for man to stumble.
Truly, everything is good, but from our heart springs the trouble.
Now, God cannot be tempted, nor does he tempt any man,
but we are our own undoing as the fire that we fan…
We are led astray by our desires and enticed by our sin,
which we have fashioned in our hearts to be the glory of men.
A man was given free will to be whatever he wants to be,
and they say that you *are* whatever you want to eat…
I guess that man has finally figured that since he won't be himself
he'll lose all faith in God and that he might as well eat himself…
But the scientists are dead wrong, just as wrong as the cannibals,
we are born of God; we did not come from animals!

Yeah, it's a dog-eat-dog world; abortion is publicly approved!
In the name of science, we eat each other as food…
Population control is now a global disaster;
just let the cannibals loose, and the people will die faster!
Why hide behind science and say that it's scientifically proven
just to justify sin and the free will we are abusing…?
They say that we come from apes, but even the monkeys know
that science is just a cover for the sinful the seeds that we sow;

that in a world of corruption and greed, on each other, we feed,
instead of looking inside ourselves for the strength that we need.
Starving in a world where the food grows out of the ground;
take the soul out of a man, and now that man is on the prowl…

But the scientists are wrong, just as wrong as the cannibals,
we are born of God; we did not come from animals!

Truly, nothing that God created was meant for man to stumble.
Truly, everything is good, but from the heart springs the trouble.

No, God cannot be tempted, nor does he tempt any man,
but we are our own undoing, just as the fire that we fan.

We are led astray by our desires and enticed by our sin,
which we have fashioned in our hearts to be the glory of men.

What a wonderful creation, as every one of us 'know;'
now, shall it all go up in flames as the Atom bombs blow…

Yeah, the scientists are wrong, just as wrong as the cannibals,
we are born of God; we did not come from animals…

There is Hope for The World

Thank God almighty! There is hope for the world;
there's hope for every boy, and there is promise for every girl.
Yes, the future of our seed has a great hope indeed,
their purpose is no more bleak, but there's a point we must reach.
The reason for all mankind has led up to this;
to the hope of the world, to the end we shall exist!
Let their lights shine bright, let their vision be clear,
and let the sun be in their hearts to overcome their darkest fears.
God's creation took him patience; we still await the day it's complete.
We were brought to life by his word; now, shall we die at his feet?
Surely, his love has never changed; his heart won't miss a beat.
But when all is said and done, are we too angry to see?
Yes, one day, we'll learn to love unconditionally;
once our hearts reach conditions we are unable to see...

The World Needs Love

The fact that there's poverty on a planet where the food grows out of the
ground is preposterous, and a shame to us all, as a human race, until now...
I could see if there was poverty on a desert planet like Mars;
I could see if there were starving things on a cold planet, like Pluto, but
ours??
We are sustaining of life; we are not where life cannot sustain,
but the fact that the earth has poverty is a testament to our very self-evident
pain.
In the Bible, God would cause famines; yes, he would withhold the rain.
If there was injustice in the land, he would make known our shame.
So that we could see that from the heavens he sees poverty lying within us,
he would starve the earth, the ground he'd curse, and water would never
replenish.
Yes, he'd hold back the rain, we'd suffer in pain;
but he only did it for 'reason'...
See, with water all gone, our reason grew strong,
and we'd beg for a change and forgiveness...
But if salt loses its savor, wherewith shall it be salted,
and if this world die at the core, shall heaven be finally exalted?
The truth is that we have all we need; no, our need is not all we have.
But at the heart of the matter, we desire disaster,
forsaking the number one task...
Surely, as dew covers the ground, surely, as rain ascends from above,
we need not more ground to stand, but our world simply needs love...

Bullies eventually Get Bullied

Remember back in the day when, if you had 'the juice,'
you wound up getting into one fight, and that one fight turned into two?
It seemed like everyone wanted a piece of you after that so that they could
be king of the hill...
Violence begets more violence; Martin Luther King could see it was
misdirected zeal...

Bullies, eventually, get bullied: if there's one thing that reigns supreme,
it's 'that'!

Violence may seem to overcome you, but violence shall not overcome you;
that's fact...
Hold onto your innocence, hold on to your meekness;
let patient endurance reside in your heart!
The violent may call weakness
what you perceive to be smart...

because bullies, eventually, get bullied...

I know you wonder when it will stop:
the senseless killings, the injustice; all for the sake of being on top...
How many 'innocent' have to die before weapons we finally drop?

There will always be someone bigger, stronger, and faster;
there will always be someone better...
but what is bronze to brains;
what are bars to chains;
eventually, we become clever
and realize...
that bullies, eventually, get bullied...

Passion

Shattered remains left
of the window with stains.
A charred wooden deck
after hours of flames:
from the pews, now views
of the seasons of change.
its wood grow rotten
after seasons of rain...

Creaky old steps
to where the choir would sing.
Ants run rapid a rusted tambourine.
Not a lot has happened
since the talk of the town,
not a lot of passion
since it burned to the ground...

World War

The timid will not survive
as resilient worlds collide.
From differences of opinion
springs knowledge of division
creating a world of conflict
in which worlds find collision.

It's a world war!

Ideals combine and clash,
realities shift and shake,
bend and brake as forces smash;
home invasions steel the peace,
the innocent kneel as prey
holding fast to the new world
as the old world wastes away!

Sins Blind a Man

Sins blind a man until you can't find a man;
if you knew better, you'd do better,
but you can't see past your own righteousness...

Oh, what skill it takes to remain teachable.
Humility is real; it makes you remain reachable,
but pride will blind you to the point where you can't find 'you'...

At what point exactly does a hope become bleak:
only when there is sin in the way that you seek.

Indeed, sins blind a man until you can't find a man;
if you knew better, you'd do better,
but you can't see past your own righteousness.

Like the Terminator on judgment day
or a nuclear holocaust that wipes tears away,
with the peak of civilization as high as this
the pride of man shall not exist...
because sins blind a man until you can't find a man:
if you knew better, you'd do better,
but you can't see past your own righteousness...

The error of his way causes him to go further astray.
His heart doesn't survive in him, but it dies in him...
With meekness confused as weakness,
now, strong is the pride in him!
Troubles more than the hairs of his head,
he can't think his way out of this;

issues so complicated,
to the end that he can't exist...
because sins blind a man until you can't find a man;
if you knew better, you'd do better,
but you can't see past your own righteousness...

It's Just a Matter of Time

If nothing else moves you,
let this change ya mind:
the fact of the matter is
it's just a matter of time...

there's a lot of truth to the saying
ignorance is bliss;

wisdom dwells with prudence,
so, get it while time permits...

Don't wait till the last minute
to make *eternal* decisions,

blissful as you are
you cannot remain ignorant...

Something is on its way,
and you are on your way to something;

believe me when I say,
there's no way that it's nothing!

If nothing else moves you,
let this change ya mind:

the fact of the matter is
it's just a matter of time!

Does The Sun Hurt Your Eyes?

Be honest with yourself,
does the sun hurt your eyes?
Do you welcome the rays in,
or do you let down the blinds;
are you elated or frustrated;
do you love it, or do you hate it?

What would you say...?
At the dawn of civilization,
how will you greet the day?
Do you love the nighttime;
do you go out when it's dark?
Are you working to keep a secret;
are you hiding inside your heart?

Should the truth be exposed
would it have you surprised?
Is your awakening rude;
does the sun hurt your eyes?

America is Standing on a Giant Trap

America is standing on a giant trap;
oh, what a hollow ground we stand!
one false move and it might crack,
so beware the master's plan…
Tread lightly, America,
because although there is hope for where we're at,
we mustn't lie; lest we die we can't deny the facts;
we are skating on the thinnest ice
America is standing on a giant trap!

As our foundation die within us, only a shallow shell remain.
Upon feeble crust, we stand aloof to the depth of all our pain.
Our foundation would fall beneath our feet
the day we bare our shame.
Our pride is high, but lest we die
we must not stay the same.
Truth be told, as sure as gold,
only the meek can make us whole.
We must set our hands to a humble work;
we must now secure our soul!
No longer should we praise our name
nor lift our soul with hope so vain,
but it is now that we must repent,
it is now that we must change.

As yet, so proudly, we proclaim the crust
while a sinkhole lie beneath the surface.

With a mighty crash, the dust will clear as we appear imperfect.
In our fallen state, with mouth agape, do we finally fill the gap;
the empty void, a loathsome noise; America is standing on a giant trap.

When the mountains Fall

When the mountains fall,
when the valleys arise,
should you behold it
with your own two eyes,
will you know what's good for you...?

God gives, and he takes away;
truth be told, if God is your stay,
this leveling of the ground you stand
won't cause your faith to sway.

The humble will hear of it and praise the Lord;
the prideful will dread it till their hearts destroyed.

What man should fear the day all men stand equal,
but a man who is evil and sets himself above the people

He had no share in what is fair,
concerning what he should, and shouldn't do.
Now, on that day when God arrives,
will you know what's Good for you...?

From the glory of his awesome presence, the mountain tops smoke
as an inspiring fire kindles in the valley of the humbleness of hope.

Arise oh barren valleys, stand upright in your posture.
You were sick, but now you're healed
in the presence of your doctor.
Mourning has had its day,

but now rejoice, you are the light!
Remove the shadow of the mountain,
and you shall now regain your sight.

Oh, prideful man, oh lifted up, the wicked exult because of you,
but vanity is a vain pursuit; now see what will become of you.

You made your home in the heavens,
now your grave is grounds for the poor.

Indeed, they shall stand upright,
but you shall stand no more.

The World's Last Judge

He is easily misconstrued,
even thought to be deceptive.
In the world by which he's viewed,
he must maintain his directive.
He stands alone, it seems;
so many peers have left him.
In view of all his dreams,
this world can't help reject him.

When your decisions truly conflict
with the way society shapes you
you are detested and tested as if God himself should hate you.
But on the contrary, you are a testament
to the contradictions of the world.
You resonate in the minds of those
whose true hope unfurls.
They deny this conflict, the true condition of their heart,
but you display this conflict as though it were an art.
They quickly pass judgment on you to ensure their peace of mind,
but you withhold your judgment, aware of their true design.
For such a generation as this, you were brought into creation;
to stand opposite of the world, to speak of its devastation.
You will die a lonely death, a lonely death you must die,
for you were born with such hope, that many sorrows multiply.

Your demonstration of desolation is the way we must all go;
a living sacrifice to end the world as we know.
It's no surprise that they don't understand you

and don't care for your calling.
It's no surprise that you'll be standing
in the midst of their falling.
They desecrate your name, no doubt it's all in vain;
for their only hope is in you to arouse them of their shame.

Hold true your conviction, stand by your decision;
you are not alone, trust in your provision.
The world is behind you, now lead them in love.
They may seek, but will not find you:
the world's last judge.

The Wise will be Waiting

So, whenever you get through hating,
open your eyes and realize
the wise will be waiting.
I know how strongly you feel
about how wrongly they deal,
but some things time must reveal.
Fret not, don't worry, be still;
the wise will be waiting.
If you consider yourself to be smart,
be careful to take this to heart:
May the hope of your love not depart.
Be patient, oh light in the dark;
the wise will be waiting.
Genius is unending patience.
I know what they do is outrageous;
love will make you courageous
to stand against hate so contagious.
So, whenever your through with your hating,
please open your eyes and realize
the wise will be waiting.
I know how strongly you feel
about how wrongly they deal.
Fret not, don't worry, be still!
The end that they meet shall reveal
the wise have been waiting.

The Day the World Hates Love

There is a reason why they say
'don't look for love in the club.'
Because in the club they worship money
and for money, people will show no love.

Must be a reason why every artist
after their first cd drop,
in order to go gold or platinum, eventually, turn pop.

As if life is a big ol' party and the world is a giant club
where there is no need for a sorry
cause there's no real desire for love

At the "end of the world parties," the drug will have to be intense
to make you super delusional to take away the very real suspense

Ecstasy will now be why-to-see,
in the club with shades so dark
that finally, we'll go blind to see.
Because as a whole, we're really not going anywhere,
which means we're going nowhere fast.
As a result, "Are we there yet?"
will become more frequently asked…
On a road trip to God knows where,
only God knows where on this road we trip.
Yet we blame God till the end of it;
in our last days, we'll only hope to quit.

It's no wonder why love is a scarcity
and the family is so rare to see.

At this point, the whole we've dug
assures our fate a deadly drug.
We long await the moons of blood
the day the world needs love.

Is it Written?

The line is long, and inside, my heart is smitten;
as I approach the throne of God, I long to know:
"Is it written...?"
I was foretold of this day on earth,
that one day we would give an account of our lives,
that he would open a book to find our name,
to determine who lives and who dies…
So, "Is it written…?"
A daunting question I wish I'd asked long ago.
On earth, Bibles were easy to find; still, the truth, I dared not to know…
I skipped Sunday School, and I slept through Pastor's lesson.
All the while, he spoke from this book, but I never thought to question:
"Is it written…?
Is it written of me in the scroll?"
Like a child with an awkward name awaiting the teacher's call of the role:
"Is it written…?
Is it written of me in the book?
Is my name in the book of life which, on earth, I dared not to look?

Is the law of God in my heart; in my heart, is there the law of God?"
A question I wish I'd have asked long ago before this day had arrived…

I'm drawing closer now to the throne, and my heart pounds deep within me.
To discover now the unknown has left my spirit and soul so empty…
there are two in front of me now; I stand but two name-calls away,
to know my place for eternity; if from a book, my name he should say…

Yes, many are called, but few are chosen:
many are called, but very few choose
to hear the calling of God,
to apply their heart to these rules…

What is the law of God?
Oh, how I wish it were now in my heart;
to know if my name be found,
and the end to which I depart…
"Is it written…?"
The line is long, and inside, my heart is smitten;
as I approach the throne of God,
I long to know,
"Is it written…?"

CHAPTER 12

The World Upside Down

The Peculiar People

There's something about this 'people,'
something very peculiar.
We see them time and time again,
yet they remain unfamiliar.
Why is their duty estranged to us;
why are we aloof of their mission?
What is it about this 'people'
that rings with division?
Though they look the same as us,
somehow, they're still different,
for they be outcast amongst us
as pilgrims with pro-visions.
Their appearance is often ghastly
as one not in tune with the seasons:
They dress themselves as though
they have their own reasons…
Their logic does confuse us
for their way is not our way;
we look with scorn upon them,
but they don't care the things we say.
I can't help but wonder
if our Good is their evil,
for they oppose this very world
and set themselves
peculiar people…

That Is the Hope We Share

We walk amongst the lilies,
we dance through dandy lions 'fair';
prancing fields of glory,
we have not cares to bear!
Daisies are as due drops,
beware the tulip's glare,
for the grounds we stand are gorgeous,
that is the hope we share...

What a beautiful sight is the concrete rose:
we push a cart and dodge potholes;
we walk in shoes that show our toes;
we lay our head where no one knows.

In the trash heap, we find what's buried;
where rodents run, and rats do scurry.
We find our wait where others hurry;
we walk the streets, our clothing dirty...

What a dreadful sight, they say
as they see the grounds we stand.
Yes, so many passers-by
wish not be dealt our hand

But let time tell it,
behold the truth in grains of sand,
our hour has yet to come;
beware the master's plan...

For we walk amongst the lilies,
we dance through dandy lions 'fair';
prancing fields of glory
we have not cares to bear!
Daises are as due drops,
beware the tulip's glare,
for the grounds we stand are gorgeous,
that is the hope we share.

Estranged of Men

There is a reason why, at times, I find myself my only friend.
As if I am a stranger to the world;
the world is a stranger to the world within.

Dare I follow my heart, dare, on my heart, I should depend,
I will find myself a loner in this world, and estranged of men.
Lean on your imagination, and you'll, most likely, go against the grain.
In exchange for your heart's true desire,
your flesh must endure the pain!
Most men seek only to be ordinary,
few there be who truly seek to change.
Now, as for the man who follows his heart,
truly, he seeks to be estranged.
To move forward in a world of men who so willfully go backward.
Of a truth, he can't afford a friend:
as a stranger to the world;
the world is a stranger to the world within.
Dare I follow my heart; dare on, my heart, I should depend,
I will find myself alone in this world;
in this world estranged of men.

Poor Blind Sheep

Poor blind sheep, indeed, the truth is deep!
The truth of who you are is the cost of what you keep.
You don't know that they may use you,
but you know that they'd accuse you:
the peer pressure of wolves is only meant to confuse you.
In a top-secret plot to take over the world,
you are the blind sheep as the plan unfurls...
You catch a sheep with a sheep, so they use you as bait
but they can only use you if your purpose is fake...
Now, you are in disguise, and shade covers your eyes:
a sheep in wolf's clothing now that's a surprise...

Everything Is Nothing to Me

Everything is nothing to me;
money, cars, and clothes are just something to see,
but for real, everything is nothing to me.
If I build a house on a hill, how long will it be;
everything is just dust eventually.
The richest man is poor, and the poorest man is rich,
but we don't see it that way because it's something that we cannot get.
Trying to hold on to things is like grasping thin air;
we have all that we need, but can't see that it's right there.
What lies on the inside is all we can count;
what's beyond our control is to what we amount.
Yeah, money, cars, and clothes are just something to see,
but every heart knows that eventually
the only thing that matters is the thing that we 'be.'
Therefore, everything is nothing to me.
And if all is nothing, then what more is everything
than an illusion for confusing the soul of every being.

Everything Is Fading at The Crust

Everything is fading at the crust:
everything, decaying and corroding into dust.
There's nothing really on the surface; you can count it all worthless;
everything is fading at the crust...
The lilies of the valley last a day
as the beauty of a flower fades away,
there's nothing really on the surface made to stay,
so why sell out for a dream, why be gay?
What is man but a vapor in the wind;
a flash in the pan, a grain of sand, mere men?
Our claim to fame is the dust that descends.
There's nothing really on this earth, so what's the fuss,
truly everything is fading at the crust...
Who has excellent hearing and 2020 vision?
The real blind and death of this world just lack conviction.
The pride of life has blinded so many living on the surface,
materialism has made their hearing and seeing worthless.
They have become worthless as the items they worship;
fashioned in God's image, they downgrade for the appearance of perfect.
They want the newest and latest version of the same old nothing...
As the hope of their eye dims
the light of their soul fades away,
and with each passing day
the beauty of their reality slowly turns to grey.
So long they've been black and white...
"I call 'em how I see em," they say,
but an eye for an eye takes the magic away
from the start of a day.
But should the sun go down on your wrath,
the setting of the sun would have no array.

The American Dream Must Die

The American Dream must die!
Ain't no sense in wondering why!
We put enough time and energy into it
to Finally see that the point that we prove is foolish.
It took a long time for me to see
that God would never be lifted on earth;
that this is truly Satan's kingdom,
upon which God's people are cursed.
But let me be the first one to tell it;
let me be the one to say it first:
We are on a futile mission
to think heaven could ever be earth!
The American dream must die,
the pride of life is a lie,
though only the humble will see it,
it takes 'real-eyes' to believe it!
This here is a figment of our imagination;
our imagination without restraint.
We figure that we are painting the perfect picture,
but a perfect picture, we cannot paint...
The American Dream must die!
This life is a life of illusion;
everyone dreams to go up,
when it's all going down in confusion...

It seems morbid; it seems quite be bleak;
it seems melancholy, the way that I seek,
but if the truth is what we should teach,

then prosperity, I'll never preach!
So, I'll preach to the truth, till the chalkboard board screech, I'll preach!
Like silverware on fine China, I'll squall, and I'll squeak!
Yes, I'll preach to the smite of one's hand, to the turning of both cheeks!
I'll teach until nails go through my hands;
until nails go through my feet, I'll preach…
The American Dream must die!

Honor The Fallen Heroes

Prevent the humiliation of the proud by the proud being humbled:
respect their struggle;
and honor the fallen heroes.
We can save ourselves as a world by uplifting the humbled.
Why look down on those whose strength has crumbled?
We should honor the fallen heroes…

Pay respect to whom respect is due.
See, the humble see the hoops which the proud must go through;
they know all too well, and there is much to be gained
in the pride of our shell: the example of shame…
Yes, we must honor the fallen heroes…
though we look on them with scorn, our heart should be torn;
for every hero that has fallen is a nation reborn!
I say we honor the fallen heroes…
Be careful who you despise, not to count them as zeros,
lest who you call out a coward, God calls out a hero.
There is much meaning to their life and great depth to their soul;
should we inquire of the fallen, their glory, we would uphold.
We must honor the fallen heroes…
In their way is life, although we only see their death;
they perish upon the earth for reasons that we forget…
I say we honor the fallen heroes!
One day we will need their courage, to know the truth of their story,
to know the strength that it took to stand; although their shame be our
glory,
we must honor the fallen heroes…
Yes, we must uplift them from the place which they stand!

How do we know that their fall wasn't planned,
that the purpose to their life isn't grand,
that in 'hu-man-ity' they are the 'man'...?
I say we honor the fallen heroes!

The Shame of the Nation

He is the shame of the nation,
the reason for all discontent.
Oh, what sorrow assails him
in their need to repent…
His story is their destruction;
to them, he is an obstruction,
while as yet, a moral compass
to make known their corruption.
He kept not silent his convictions,
but cried out in the streets!
Shouting their devastation
till the gritting of teeth.
They did not know what to do with him;
they writhed in frustration
while beholding their guilt:

the shame of the nation…

"Should the whole nation be cast down
by one man and his God?"
"But if he be right, then we shall die in our pride…."

Trouble

His presence is far from subtle,
so everywhere he goes, he brings trouble.
Stirring the waters of reason,
tempers flare as tension bubbles.
Before him, the truth could stay hidden;
now at his showing, the truth is alive.
As for those walking in darkness,
he is troubling unto their eyes.
Before he came, they could not
see themselves clearly,
their eyes droopy and dreary.
Oh, what hideous monsters lurk in the dark,
imbittered in chains ever weary.
Now at his appearance, they scoff, and they scorn,
for he is a beast in their sight.
As children of darkness will always abhor
anything born of the light.
His influence is too much for them,
there is power in every rebuttal;
his presence alone is haunting them
his being is far from subtle.

There is a fear of being discovered;
of being set free, the fear is doubled.
Now, everywhere that he goes,
it is said that he brings trouble.

CHAPTER 13

Perfect Love

Paradox

I can't really define this relationship of a divine dimension;
as my head ponders the paradox, my feet float in suspension.
He reveals to me that the things weighing me down aren't worth clenching;
now loose from the grasp of my past, I begin my ascension!

Never have I ever beheld a beauty so bold and so bright;
a love so uplifting, so deserving of life!
Resistance is futile; I feel unworthy to fight;
the innocence of infancy is the plea of my plight
seeing that I am but a baby before his power and might...

As in the hands of my creator, I place my security and my trust,
I arise from the ashes; vividly, I appear from the dust.
With a gust of wind, he blows away the sand and the crust
declaring me free from sin, born again through the spirit of love...

"You're new," he says,
"go your way and be free, but remember, no matter where you go, in your
heart, I'll always be...."
"Be true," he says,
"for a lie is never of me. But remember, no matter what you do, I love you
unconditionally!"

With my new form and renewed strength, I open my eyes and awake
to find myself crouched bedside, hands folded in place.
I can't really define this relationship of a divine dimension;
as my head ponders the paradox, my feet float in suspension...
He reveals to me that the things weighing me down aren't worth clenching;
now loose from the grasp of my past, I begin my ascension!

The Perfect Mirror

God is the perfect mirror from which to see.
When we view ourselves through this mirror,
we view ourselves perfectly.
Lacking in no way, perfect in our perception;
God makes clear as day the beauty of our reflection.

If only we could see ourselves the way that he sees,
he would reveal to us his glory placed inside of our being,
he would show to us the standard for which we marvel creation;
the beauty found in eyes both loving and patient.

We come alive at his work, at the beauty we see,
looking into a mirror that views perfectly.

But that he loves us to perfection,
Nothing's ever been clearer;
that we are perfect in every way,
staring into the perfect mirror...

I Plead the Blood

As I stand trial today,
as you state your case against me,
I try to justify all the evil that is in me.
In my search for justice,
each time, I return empty
for I am bloody from head to toe,
even my soul has need of cleansing!
In desperation for hope,
in a feeble attempt at love,
I have but one defense, your honor
and that is, I plead the blood!
The only case I have today,
the only reason your time be lost,
is that someone has done my time,
therefore, my crime should have no cost...
Do as you see fit;
by all means, my life is in your hands.
But know that your judgment of me
shall be how *your judgment stands...*
Although I badly deserved to die,
someone goodly has died for me.
So, as you consider what my life is worth,
don't forget that I am free!
They stretched him long, they stretched him wide;
they beat him red, they hung him high.
They pierced a sword into his side,
and out spilled blood: my reason why...
I plead the blood...

Love Without Conditions

Christ lives in all of us
and all of us live in Christ,
because a love without limits
is a love that has life…

I'll say that again…

Christ lives in all of us
and all of us live in Christ,
because a love without limits
is a love that has life…

Allow me to go a little deeper…
if you will, please grant me the permission
to expound upon a love
that has no condition…
You see, its form is so unsightly
the human eye cannot absorb
a passion shining so brightly
that it makes the eyes sore…

So, the fact of the matter is
it simply cannot be seen…
it exists only in our hearts,
lives solely in our dreams.
Still, its power is very present
for we feel its warmth upon our skin
and though it be billions of miles away
we hear its call from deep within.

Its positioning is so perfect
in the history of time
that though it be centuries ago,
today, it still refreshes the mind.
You see, this love without conditions
is for conditions without love;
for circumstance, situations,
and people without hugs...

See, this creation is self-sustaining:
it is set up to the end;
it will always be,
and it has always been!

No, there is no real explanation,
no clear way to describe
this love that keeps living
just to keep us alive...

When we attempt to grasp its glory
we fail to envision
a love without limits;
a love without conditions...

Levels Of Compassion and Depths to Mercy

There truly are levels of compassion and depths to mercy;
where the level of my caring meets the depths you hurt me.
How easy it is to forgive a friend,
one whose love makes you complete,
but imagine the depth of love it takes
to forgive the enemy;
to endure the length of suffering required for them to be whole
without knowledge of the pain they bear in the depths of their soul.
Long-suffering finds new meaning
as compassion meets new levels.
They say God's mercy has no limits;
a love to deep for shovels.
Where human eyes would go blind
before They begin to see or understand
the mastery of such compassion,
where mercy has no plan.
With no guarantee of your rise
in the face of defeat, could you stand;
to the turning of both cheeks,
to the smite of one's hand?
Truly there's only one man that I know
who would fight for my soul till the end.
He died for his enemies,
now he is more than a friend.
Surely, I'll find him standing there,
where the level of my caring meets the depths you hurt me.
Truly,
there are levels of compassion and depths to mercy...

Know Your Worth

Based on the mistakes you've made, this world would throw you away
yet, you wake up every morning blessed with another day...
As the planet orbits the sun, another day has begun
and the universe disagrees with what other people say...
So, know your worth...

Because what is right with you far outweighs what is wrong;
know your worth...

You've made mistakes, but none are more than the value of who you are;
know your worth...

don't be swayed by those who accuse you, Love,
today the birds sang you a song;
Know your worth...

for there was one who paid, with blood,
the cost for all that's wrong...
So, know your worth...

Printed in the United States
by Baker & Taylor Publisher Services